A SUCCESSFUL STATE OF MIND

WENDY BRUMWELL

Published in 2022 by Discover Your Bounce Publishing

www.discoveryourbouncepublishing.com

Copyright © Discover Your Bounce Publishing

ISBN 978-1-914428-08-1

Page design and typesetting by Discover Your Bounce Publishing

TESTIMONIALS

"I am so grateful to have you as my mentor as you have been amazing. You show me the courage to do things and the attitude of never giving up which is so important in my journey"

Jayne Wong

"Wendy's approach was holistic and contextualised, taking into consideration many broad aspects of starting and running a business. Her sessions concentrated on true infrastructure; personal health and life-goals"

Pepper Barney

DEDICATION

This book is dedicated to my amazing family who always believe in me and offer endless love and support.

My loving husband, Ross Brumwell, for his belief and encouragement.

My beautiful mum, Maureen Day, for always being there for me.

My charming dad in heaven, Henry Day, for the poem that inspired me.

The best in laws ever, Sue and Dave Brumwell for their wise words.

My gorgeous boy, Lucca the lab, for the dog walks that gave me so many ideas!

CONTENTS

INTRODUCTION

Have you ever wondered why professional sportspeople seem to transition so well from a career as an athlete to other vocations, often becoming entrepreneurs, business leaders or business owners? What is it about a sportsperson that makes them successful? Were they born 'special', is it just natural talent, or is it their 'state of mind,' often referred to as mindset? I personally like to use 'state' rather than 'set' as a state refers to a condition that someone is in at a particular time, but this state can move and grow rather than implying a set or fixed position.

You may have read many books on how to get started in business, leadership, entrepreneurship or investing. Perhaps you have gained a great deal of knowledge, read about how to start a business or how to invest, but have you received the results that you expected? Did you take action? Well, no one could argue that it's important to get educated and know how to start and scale a business. However, from my experience and research, this only accounts for a small percentage of what is required to succeed. What you may be missing is the bigger part of the equation, the all-important state of mind, that can help you take action to reach your goals, get results and make the difference to what you achieve. The successful state of mind that will help you on your journey to create your version of success.

One of the reasons you may have bought this book is because you believe that it will help you understand more about how professional sportspeople, and in fact all sportspeople, operate mentally. You can then apply this state of mind to your business and your life to help you be more successful. Although there are many books that give valuable knowledge about entrepreneurship and mindset, I have not found a book that specifically targets the principles you will find in this book, taken directly from sport and applied to business. This book does not focus on the technical knowledge to start and grow a business, but instead focuses primarily on the state of mind required to succeed.

The success stories you may have read on mindset, business, and entrepreneurship usually come from a person who has achieved their success, tells their story, and shares their wisdom to help you do the same. After all, it worked for them, so if you follow their special formula then exactly the same will work for you. That's where there is a gap. We are all individuals and therefore have different states of mind. This means that we need to apply a 'state of mind' that will work well for us as individuals. So the question is, what is required to be successful in our business? I don't believe it's a special quality or magic potion and I don't think it comes overnight, but I do believe anyone can do it with the principles outlined in this book. These principles offer you the opportunity to design your own unique journey and achieve your version of success. Further, they can all be learned and applied to your business in a way that's right for you. We were not born with these principles; they are not innate. We can all develop them to help us take action to be successful. You can do it, but it is up to you; I don't believe everyone will do this. Why not? Read on, you will find out as you read this book.

How Has Professional Sport Helped in My Property Business?

I am a professional figure skating coach and successful property entrepreneur. I believe there is a very strong correlation between these two in terms of state of mind. Not only do I have experience of professional sport and entrepreneurship, but I have also started from scratch and have been what you might call down, dirty, and hands-on with both. I've experienced the highs, the lows and the rejection. The wins, positives, negatives, and many failures, challenges, and frustrations. I have lived each day since the age of seven in the world of sport, which required a high level of dedication at such a young age. I was taught by world and Olympic champions and trained with many very successful world-class international and British competitors. As a professional coach for fifteen years, I trained many young athletes and have spent many years researching and studying what makes the difference on whether we are successful or not.

I was a high-level figure skater, competing nationally and internationally. This sportsperson lifestyle I experienced, combined with many years of extensive research studying the qualities of top athletes, taught me the principles I use today to be successful in my property business. I am eternally grateful for this experience, what it taught me, and the life lessons from sport that I could apply to being a successful property entrepreneur owning a multi-million pound portfolio. I am living my version of success by using these principles, and now I would like the opportunity to share these principles with you to help you achieve your version of success.

The principles I've learned and researched over the years in sport have given me a mental toughness that helps me every day in my property business, and they can be learned to help you be mentally tough in your business journey too. Once you have read this book, you will have learned and developed all the state of mind principles to help you be successful and, be able to identify the principles that require the most work. You can then focus your attention on these areas to help you succeed. There are exercises at the end of each chapter to help you develop your state of mind, and these can be repeated as many times as you require. Each exercise has been specifically designed to reinforce the lessons in this book and help develop your state of mind to be successful. You can download a free electronic version of the all the exercises and templates in the State Of Mind Playbook, at www.stateofmindplaybook.com.

How Does My Experience Help?

I am writing this book having been a professional figure skater and coach, a successful property business owner, a university graduate, and a certified coach and mentor. Moreover, I have conducted extensive research of the sportsperson mindset. I have studied many top athletes, my own mindset from sport to business, the successful qualities of entrepreneurs and the top principles that all these people share that can be learnt and tailored to us as individuals. I certainly haven't written this book without any experience, research and knowledge. I have built a property business from the ground up, so I know what it's like to start out.

I also know what it's like and what is required to be successful in both sport and business. I've coached many talented young athletes, been surrounded by elite athletes and I've worked with many successful property entrepreneurs and business owners. Moreover, I've met many great athletes that haven't had the success they desire and met many unsuccessful property investors and business owners that have all the knowledge and don't take action. From analysing their behaviour, I found that they are all good people with good intentions, who may be intelligent, talented, and really want to do well, but there is that something that holds them back.

This is exactly what we are going to explore further in this book. The state of mind principles you can learn and apply that will help you achieve your potential in business and entrepreneurship, master your thoughts and beliefs, own your money state of mind, and advance your results with focused effort.

Asking the Question, 'What Makes the Difference?'

I started asking the question, 'what makes the difference?' many years ago whilst coaching figure skating and starting my property business. Why will one person win a competition, while an equally capable athlete won't? Why does one property investor buy lots of property and experience success while others, despite having all the same knowledge, just can't seem to start their first project? This is where state of mind is so important for anything you want to achieve, in business and in life. So many people have all the knowledge and skill to succeed, but they just don't have the right state of mind to take action.

As I mentioned, there is no magic here, but from my many years of experience, knowledge, and in-depth research, I will let you know what I believe makes the difference. I will also tell you how you can apply the principles I've learned in a way that is right for you. This is not about what has worked for me. This is about you and what works for you. The way you use these principles and do the exercises will give you your own answers. The only request I make is that you read the principles in order, as there are some dependencies that you will note when you read through the book.

The Secret!

The BIG secret is… there is no secret to get success. However, by believing in your state of mind, learning and applying the principles in this book, I really believe you can unlock the secret to whatever success means to you and achieve it with focused, consistent effort.

So, let's get started with first understanding more about why sportspeople make great entrepreneurs, my sports background, and how I not only learnt these principles from my experience in sport, but also researched and developed them to apply successfully to entrepreneurship and business.

CHAPTER ONE

WHAT MAKES SPORTSPEOPLE GREAT ENTREPRENEURS?

From extensive research into the minds of sportspeople, I strongly believe that the qualities which enable them to achieve success in their chosen field are largely the same qualities that are essential to be successful as an entrepreneur. The characteristics that help athletes win competitions and keep on going despite the challenges that they face, are the exact same ones required to be successful in the entrepreneurial world of business, or to reach the top of any industry for that matter. Being an entrepreneur can be a very challenging and emotional rollercoaster, but sportspeople have a head start because they have already learned these state of mind principles that are perfect for achieving success as an entrepreneur.

I would describe sport as the school of life, as it teaches great values such as personal improvement, being goal-oriented, determination, resilience, managing emotions and how to perform well under pressure. Every successful athlete knows how to overcome challenges and understands that in order to succeed, you must work smart and never stop improving and learning.

Sportspeople have a passion for their sport and this passion is what drives them to keep going and make it through the tough times. In these tough times a sportsperson will not give up, even when faced with failure. An athlete has a clear vision of themselves as being successful and they will map out a path to achieve that vision. This vision also needs self-belief or self-confidence and those athletes who have self-belief are the ones who will have the highest success. The same is true for entrepreneurship.

To illustrate this point, let's look at some examples of highly successful and famous sportspeople who have also achieved fantastic results when making the transition to business or entrepreneurship.

Case Studies

Venus Williams

A great example of a very highly accomplished sportswoman who is now a successful entrepreneur is the inspirational Venus Williams. She has won a staggering 7 Grand Slam singles tennis titles and 14 Grand Slam doubles titles (at the time of writing). Venus is also the owner of VStarr Interiors (an interior design company) and the founder/CEO of athletic wear brand EleVen.

In an interview with CNBC, Venus Williams stated that the skills she learned and developed in sport were the same that made her successful in business.

"Sport is so much like business. It's all about strategy. And it's all about learning from losing. It's all about setting goals."

Venus Williams

Venus Williams is not the only sportsperson to be successful in business. Let's look at a few more examples.

Derek Jeter

Derek Jeter was a world series winning New York Yankee shortstop who is now the CEO and co-owner of the Miami Marlins, co-founder of The Players' Tribune, founder of Jeter Publishing and founder of The Turn 2 Foundation.

"I can't always expect to be the best at everything, but I don't ever want to end a day feeling like I didn't give all I could toward whatever I faced that day."

Derek Jeter

George Foreman

George Foreman, a heavyweight champion boxer, who is most well-known for his business venture, the George Foreman Grill, signed a reported nine-figure contract in 1999 with Salton Inc., which is now Spectrum Brands, to have the naming rights of his grill. George Foreman is also the author of many cook books!

———

"My message when I speak to groups is: you're an American. And no one can take that from you. This whole country was built in someone's garage. You can achieve whatever you want."

George Foreman

———

Kobe Bryant

Kobe Bryant had a long and successful career as a shooting guard with the Los Angeles Lakers. When he retired from sport, Kobe Bryant set up an investment firm, Bryant Stibel, with businessman Jeff Stibel. He used this company to invest in large companies such as Alibaba, Dell, and Epic Games (the company behind the very popular Fortnite video game). He was also the founder of Granity studios, a multimedia company that enabled him to produce 'Dear Basketball,' which later became an Oscar-winning short film. Unfortunately, his life ended suddenly in a tragic helicopter crash when he was just 41, so he was not able to pursue his desire and visions further to get into the entertainment industry.

———

"I'll do whatever it takes to win games, whether it's sitting on a bench waving a towel, handing a cup of water to a teammate, or hitting the game-winning shot."

Kobe Bryant

———

David Lloyd

David Lloyd found business success once he had retired from tennis. Here in the UK, most of us are familiar with the upmarket David Lloyd leisure clubs that feature indoor tennis court facilities. David Lloyd was a professional tennis player who retired in 1981. The highlight of his tennis career was a semi-final Wimbledon doubles match in 1973, and as a singles player, his top rank was 128 in the world. As we can see, he was at an elite level in the sport of tennis and also a successful business owner.

The David Lloyd company has been very successful in the UK and in 1995, Whitbread PLC bought his company for a reported £200 million.

Kristi Yamaguchi

Kristi Yamaguchi was a figure skater who won the Olympic gold medal in 1992, and she is now the main entrepreneur behind the fashion brand Tsuya. Her brand sells clothes and accessories with some of the profits set aside for the Always Dream Foundation to help educate children. With a reported net worth of around £8 million, this makes her one of the highest-paid female athletes.

Todd Stottlemyre

Todd Stottlemyre was a professional baseball player who played 15 seasons in major league baseball and was a World Series champion in 1992 and 1993. Research shows that he believes failure is a huge part of success and has learned many valuable lessons from playing professional baseball.

As a businessman, Todd is a business coach, business owner and keynote speaker. He helps people to achieve their visions and goals by providing road maps to get them from where they are now to where they want to be. His baseball journey taught him to learn from failure, and he passes this on to other people, motivating them to get up when they fall and to keep going to achieve their goals.

Maria Sharapova

Maria Sharapova was a former Russian professional tennis player who, at just 18, became the world's female number one and the first Russian female to be at the top of the singles ranks.

As a businesswoman, she generated millions of dollars throughout her years on court by combining her ability, beauty and attractive personality to further her brand by partnering with and endorsing many big companies, including Nike, Evian, and Canon. She also founded a global 'guilt-free' confectionary line in 2013 called Sugarpova.

Patrick J. Sweeney II

Patrick J Sweeney was an Olympian in rowing, finishing second in the 1996 single scull Olympic trials and winning the Royal Canadian Henley International Regatta.

Once he retired, Patrick became a fear guru, an author of a book on fear, a keynote speaker, and also appears on TV, sharing the science of fear. In 2017, his 'Talks at Google' were rated as the best talks of 2017 at the EU headquarters. His mission is to help people use fear to transform their life by using a framework based on interviews with a reported 35 leading experts from all over the world.

Patrick was the son of a first-generation Irish immigrant and became the first person in his family who graduated from college to become a multi-millionaire. He believes that he owes this to his sporting background. The lessons he learned as a sportsperson helped him be successful in life.

His top lessons from sport to business include:

1. Accountability – never being a victim. Life can happen to you or by you.

2. Using fear as fuel – champions and competitors use this in sport, and this can be applied to business and life. Visualisation, breathing exercises, and meditation work well in business.

3. Setting big long-term goals – and then a way of how to achieve them.

4. Attitude for improvement – focusing on making each day better than the one before.

Calvin Brock

Calvin Brock is a former professional boxer from the USA. He competed on the USA boxing team at the summer Olympics in 2000 as a super heavyweight. His teammates were future world champions Jermain Taylor, Jeff Lacy, and Brian Viloria. However, Calvin lost to Paolo Vidoz at this Olympics, so he just missed out on winning a medal. Later in 2006, he was featured in Ring Magazine's knockout of the year for winning against Zuri Lawrence.

As a businessman, he runs a successful company called Jack and Landlords. His contractual agreements with landlords allow them to rent their house without being required to need a tenancy deposit but still being protected for losses and damages up to the value of the first month of rent.

James 'Buster' Douglas

James Douglas, often known as "Buster," was a world heavyweight champion who totally surprised the world by beating Mike Tyson in 1990. He was by far the underdog in this event with the odds at apparently 42 to

1! After this event, Buster went on to be one of the highest-paid athletes of that year.

Moving on from boxing, he co-wrote a book called Busters Bar-B-Q: Knockout Diabetes Diet that was regularly featured on ESPN, Oprah, and Martha Stewart.

When applying the same principles of his boxing career, James' cookbook was like his fight with Mike Tyson. Buster shared that he could not find any publishing house that would publish his book. This was similar to the 42 to 1 odds for the 1990 heavyweight world championship. However, he would not let his business partner give up on it and finally ended up self-publishing. That's how he became a guest on Oprah. Buster then sold the rights to the book for six figures. Basically, he never gave up and found a way against all the odds to be successful!

Robbie Fowler

A famous sportsperson who started a property investing business is Robbie Fowler, a former footballer who played for Liverpool and who has been very successful in the UK property market since his retirement. As well as owning a property portfolio worth a reported £31 million at time of writing, he also owns other businesses, including being the co-founder of the Macca and Growler Group.

Apparently, his growing property portfolio has led some fans to sing, 'We all live in a Robbie Fowler house' to the popular tune of Yellow Submarine.

Summary

As we can see from the above case studies, there is no shortage of evidence to support the argument that sportspeople make great entrepreneurs and business owners. We now also know some of the values they have learnt from the world of sport that have been carried over and applied to entrepreneurship.

Let's take a look at my own background in sport to understand more about the state of mind I learnt as a child, and how I transferred this into the world of being a property entrepreneur.

CHAPTER TWO

———

MY STORY: SPORTSPERSON TO PROPERTY ENTREPRENEUR

My sport is figure skating, and one of the reasons I started figure skating was due to illness. The doctor advised that I started a sport to make me stronger and also help my asthma. I tried many sports and really found out what I didn't like. In swimming, I didn't like diving, and in gymnastics, I didn't like being upside down. I then saw Jane Torvill and Christopher Dean on the television and decided that I wanted to try ice-skating. My mum tried to talk me out of the idea with the help of an ice cube and a knife as props. This involved her getting a knife out of the drawer and cutting the top of the ice cube, saying, "this is what you will be balancing on," pointing to the knife, and "this is the hard slippery surface you will fall over on." Despite her theatrics, and much to her disappointment, I was in no way put off. My mum had a bad experience on the ice as a child and this

16

was really affecting her. She did not want me to hurt myself or get injured as she had been. She delayed calling the ice-rink for many months; however, I finally convinced her or perhaps forced her to take me to the ice-rink. I remember her words, "I can't take you going on about this anymore." I was so determined to go that I looked up the telephone number and sat next to her whilst she called the ice-rink. That was it, I was booked on to a beginner course.

On the day, when my mum was driving me to the rink, she re-iterated to me that I would be on my bum all the time, I wouldn't be able to stand up, and it would be unlikely I'd go back. It was weird, as I remember the words but to me, they were just words. They didn't mean anything. I was busy thinking about how excited I was and how I couldn't wait to get on the ice. I was almost expecting to get on the ice and skate like Torvill and Dean! It can't be that hard, can it? I think at six years of age, nearly seven, you imagine that you can do anything, right?

At the rink, I remember getting my dark blue public skating boots, and I was very disappointed that they weren't white. Before I even stepped on the rink, I told my mum that these skating boots would need to be white next week. She was still telling me about falling over, but I wasn't listening. I remember she stopped talking and said to me, "Are you listening to me, Wendy?" I just said, "Yes, don't worry. I'll be careful, Mum," and got away from her as fast as possible. My poor mum was probably petrified!

I remember to this day the first time I stepped onto the ice; it was like magic. I'll never forget the feeling, and I have that feeling every time I step on the ice. The noise of the blade cutting the ice, the feeling of gliding, it's just magical. I skated to the other side of the rink with no issues and was put into the second class on my first day. That was it, white skating boots were purchased that day and I never looked back.

Saturday morning skating turned into very early Saturday morning skating. Then to after school skating, to before school skating; gym, ballet, and traveling around the country competing. I loved jumping and spinning around on frozen water, as it turns out, and figure skating formed part of my recovery to be a much healthier child with a lifestyle that helps me every day even now.

Looking back at how I first stepped onto the ice, it was interesting how determined, excited, and fearless I was; how I really believed that I would be able to figure skate just fine. I contemplated why I was so infatuated with this sport and so focused on getting on that ice for the first time. Perhaps it was mind over matter. My state of mind was such that I just felt, 'I can do it!' No one could tell me otherwise, and I was going to balance on that delicate blade and glide over the ice regardless.

There was a passion to do a sport that I loved doing. I was always excited to go to the ice-rink. Even just writing this now, I can hear the sound of the razor-sharp edge cutting the ice and the sensation of gliding across the ice-rink, the wind in my hair. Spinning around in a lay backspin looking at the sky, rotating through the air and the feeling of landing a jump that I had been practising for weeks or even months. There was also that drive to be better each time, and I wanted to be the best I could be. The best version of myself. I had a competitive nature and the desire to compete nationally and internationally. Moreover, I really wanted to be a professional figure skater and figure skating coach. This passion and pursuit of a goal with a clear process of how to get there underpinned the motivation, determination, persistence, and sacrifices I made in my life. My aim was to be a high performer in a sport I loved. For some, this would have been Olympic champion, others perhaps the best at their ice-rink. This taught me that whatever your version of success is, you need to know what it is so that you have a reason to work and put the effort in to reach your goal.

Moving on from my competition days, I performed in shows, had lead roles in pantomimes, and passed on my knowledge to teach others how to figure skate by becoming a professional figure skating coach. I always wanted to be able to teach ice-skating and help other young athletes achieve their version of success. In 15 years of coaching, I taught all levels from beginner to British championship competitors.

Thanks to my background as an athlete, many years of research and working with lots of other young athletes and top professional sportspeople in the country, I've learnt a great deal about why some people achieve their goals whilst others, despite great intentions, don't. Therefore, I started to document what it is that 'makes the difference.' Of course, different people have different goals; however, this book is aimed at those who want to be successful in the entrepreneurial world, and those who have not yet reached their goals, taken action or performed well on their journey to get the success they desire.

What Makes the Difference?

We mentioned earlier about asking the question, 'what is it that makes the difference?' I've met many talented young athletes that don't succeed and many well-educated, lovely people who just can't take action to start their business. The question is, why? They all have the knowledge, skill, and technical ability to succeed.

In sport, I have found that the key lies within the state of mind of the athlete. How they practise day in, day out, what qualities they learned and developed, how determined they were, their effort, commitment and self-belief. Using figure skating as an example, did the athlete really believe that they could land a double loop jump or win a competition? Did they believe that focused, purposeful practice would lead to task mastery, and would they work hard and smart enough at this level to succeed? The same can be applied to entrepreneurship, there are just so many parallels from sport to business. Would a person believe they could start and scale a business, were they determined to succeed and would they make the sacrifices required to do so?

To finish this chapter, I'd like to share a poem that was given to me by my dad and has a special significance to me. I would carry this poem in my figure skating sports bag to all my practice sessions, competitions, and basically everywhere I went! I think it is a great summary of the state of mind that is required if you want to be successful. The poem is called 'The Man Who Thinks He Can'.

The Man Who Thinks He Can

If you think you are beaten, you are;

If you think you dare not, you don't.

If you'd like to win, but you think you can't,

It is almost a cinch you won't.

If you think you'll lose, you've lost;

For out in this world we find

Success begins with a person's will

It's all in the state of mind.

If you think you're outclassed, you are;

You've got to think high to rise.

You've got to be sure of yourself before

You can ever win the prize.

Life's battles don't always go

To the stronger or faster man;

But sooner or later the person who wins

Is the one who thinks he can!

This poem is about belief; thinking 'you can' is basically accepting that your thinking is true and that you can do it. You believe in yourself that you can achieve, and you need to believe to achieve. Now, as we mentioned earlier, we all have differing views on what success is, perhaps it's a Porsche for you or maybe having a big family, and your values (what's important to you) will determine your version of success.

CHAPTER THREE

———

STATE OF MIND

In this chapter, I am going to take a closer look at the state of mind and how it helps us to be successful. I have written this book as I observed in myself, those around me and by researching many successful people, that the difference between being successful or not wasn't about natural talent or technical ability. It also wasn't just the hard work and focused practice on its own. Ultimately, there would need to be a blend of skill with effective, focused practice and critically the right state of mind. A state of mind that has the belief to achieve a goal. Any doubts and there would be someone next in the queue who would 'think he can.'

Before we go any further, I believe that to get the most out of the coming chapters, it is important to understand more about what our state of mind is made up of and how it works on a higher level. It's worth noting that although I'm well educated and a qualified coach and mentor, I'm not a psychologist. Your state of mind is very complex, so I'm explaining the key principles I've researched, learned, developed, and coached. This is from my own experience of being a sportsperson, entrepreneur, coach and mentor, whilst being surrounded by other successful sportspeople and entrepreneurs. I will share the fundamental principles of what I have found makes a person successful, so that you can learn and apply these principles to your own business and in your life to make a difference in what you achieve. We need to understand just enough about the state of mind so that we can grow our mind in the most effective way.

This is about learning so that we can reach our potential and be the best version of ourselves. This is not about changing who we are, but believing in who we are and growing our own abilities. Would you like to be the very best version of yourself? If so, then keep reading...

Whether you are just starting out on your business journey, have learned about entrepreneurship but have not taken action yet, or even if you are a more experienced business owner, this book will help you grow your state of mind with practical applications, real-life examples, techniques, tools, and exercises. We all need knowledge, but if we have just the knowledge without the right state of mind to take action, then all that knowledge will essentially be wasted. To be successful, you need both knowledge and state of mind. This book focuses on the state of mind to be successful, so that you can unlock your thinking to achieve your business and life goals.

Your current state of mind plays a more significant role in helping you achieve your goals and be successful than you might think. Most of us focus on the 'how' to do something rather than 'what' we allow ourselves to do. The famous entrepreneur, author, philanthropist, and life coach Tony Robbins believes that only 20% of what we achieve is about skill or knowledge. Yes, just 20%! Does that surprise you? I must admit, it did surprise me when I first came across this statistic and Tony Robbins has applied it with great success.

_____

"Success in life is 80% psychology and 20% skills – what you do doesn't matter if you aren't in the right mindset."

Tony Robbins.

_____

From this statistic, you can see that your state of mind is key to what you achieve. If you have all the knowledge, but you don't have the right state of mind, it will be exponentially harder to achieve your goals. You need to believe to achieve for everything you do in life.

To understand more about our state of mind, I will next explain what aspects make up and contribute to our state of mind. You will need to know this for the principles in this book to make complete sense to you so that you can learn them, do the exercises, and most importantly, take action!

What is Your State of Mind?

Your state of mind is commonly known as your mindset. On a basic level, it is your way of thinking. As I mentioned in the introduction, I call it a 'state of' rather than 'set' because I believe our minds can move and grow in different states. It's not set in a fixed position and we should not consider it in that way if we want to be our best self.

Your state of mind is made up of thoughts and beliefs that group together to form what is called your 'thought and belief habits'. These thought habits affect how you feel, what you say and what action you take. To break this down further so that we can understand what our state of mind is made up of, it's worth just considering what exactly our thoughts, beliefs, and thought habits are.

What Are Your Thoughts?

Definition
Thought: an idea or opinion produced by thinking or occurring suddenly in the mind.

Thoughts can come into our heads in so many different ways. They can be pictures, songs, words, memories, or even ideas. We all experience thoughts; we know we have them, and we often talk to each other about our thoughts. Research carried out by Dr. Fred Luskin of Stanford University found that we have approximately 60,000 thoughts per day! That number really surprised me; I knew there was a lot going on in my head personally, but around 60,000 a day is a lot of thoughts.

What Are Beliefs?

Definition
Belief: an acceptance that something exists or is true, especially one without proof.

A belief is basically an idea or a thought that we accept to be true. This belief can be based upon mathematical principles, probabilities, your religion, or culture. It could be based on your own experiences, perhaps what other people say, or knowledge that you have gained over your lifetime. When a thought or idea is evaluated in your mind with your own sound reasoning, then this means that it is accepted as your truth and is then adopted to form part of your belief system.

So now the question, what is a belief system?

On a higher level, your belief system is a set of your own beliefs. They form the basis of your personal reality and how you make sense of the world that surrounds you. Each one of us is constantly trying to make sense of the world we live in, by forming our own opinions or making judgements about all of our situations and interactions.

When a belief becomes long-lasting based on what is most important to us, it underpins the standards to which we would like to live our lives, and the choices and decisions we make. This is when our beliefs develop into our values, and our commitment grows as we see these beliefs as being important to us. Our values can be divided into various categories such as family, career, financial, or happiness. For someone to make clear, consistent, and rational decisions, the person must be able to articulate their values clearly.

What Are Your Thought and Belief Habits?

Essentially these are a sum of all your thoughts, including the thoughts you accept as being true: your beliefs. Do you notice that you sometimes have the same thoughts over and over again? These are called thought habits. Depending on what type of thoughts these are, they can either help push you forward or hold you back.

When you have these thoughts repeatedly, they become habits and, for that reason, become invisible to you. However, once you can recognise these thoughts, it's then possible to change any negative ones into more thriving thoughts that will better serve you.

Once you can get control of your thought habits, you will find that you have more control over yourself. By organising your thoughts, you can decide what you want to achieve in your business and your life. You can plan ways to action your thoughts with applied faith and continued persistence. This is how you can become the master of your own destiny.

Growth State of Mind vs. Fixed State of Mind

Our state of mind can be either in a fixed or growth state according to research by S. Dweck, Ph.D. in her book *The New Psychology of Success; How We Can Learn To Fulfil Our Potential*. In this book she explains two contrasting states of mind:

The Fixed State of Mind: the belief that abilities such as intelligence and talent are fixed traits. That talent creates success with little or no effort required. S. Dweck, Ph.D says, "In the fixed mindset, everything is about the outcome. If you fail - or if you're not the best - it's all been wasted."

The Growth State of Mind: the belief that abilities such as intelligence and talent can be developed through focused, purposeful practice and smart hard work. That intelligence and talent can be the starting point for success. This belief means that a person will love learning new skills and will have resilience when achieving their goals. It's worth noting that nearly all successful people have these qualities.

Do you know which state of mind you have?

You can find out if you have a fixed or growth state of mind by going to exercise one at the end of this chapter. Answer the questions to help you understand more about your state of mind right now. Please be honest, as this will be the best way to help you develop so that you can be successful in your business. The results of this exercise will give you a great baseline, with some helpful ways to improve your state of mind.

Growth State of Mind

S. Dweck, Ph.D. explains that people with a growth state of mind believe they can develop and improve their abilities to be the best version of themselves. Therefore to be successful, it's important that you are open to and embrace the opportunity to learn and develop the state of mind principles outlined in this book. Believing in the growth state, supports the understanding that we can grow our state of mind and learn to be our version of successful, which I have experienced so many times for myself and others.

To support this theory, research has shown that we are not born with the state of mind principles in this book. They are not innate, meaning we can all learn and develop them to achieve more by approaching all that we do in our business journey with a growth state of mind. Whilst embracing the ways to grow your 'state' using the exercise in this chapter, you will be more open to learning the principles in this book, which will, in turn, help you to be more successful as a business entrepreneur.

S. Dweck, Ph.D. states the following about the growth mindset:

"Teaching a growth mindset creates motivation and productivity in the worlds of business, education, and sports. It enhances relationships."

The state of mind principles I have developed as a child and researched throughout my coaching years are the same ones that will help you grow your state of mind to unleash your potential, take action and get results. They will give you the tools to build upon what S. Dweck describes as a growth mindset. However, for these principles to work for you, you need to believe that you can adopt them, that talent alone is not the main factor, instead focused and purposeful practice is vital. Having this belief will mean that you can grow your state of mind.

In the words of Kilroy J. Oldster, "Life has a tendency to provide a person with what they need in order to grow. Our beliefs, what we value in life, provide the roadmap for the type of life that we experience."

The state of mind within us shapes the journey of what lies ahead of us.

EXERCISES: STATE OF MIND

Exercise #1

What statement do you agree with below, A or B?

1. **A.** I am either intelligent or dumb.

   B. I can grow and develop my intelligence.

2. **A.** Success is based on talent.

   B. Success is based on purposeful, focused effort.

3. **A.** Failure is a chance to learn and know what doesn't work.

   B. Failure means that I can't do it and I need to give up.

4. **A.** All feedback is a personal attack and dislike of me.

   B. Feedback is useful information and can help me learn.

5. **A.** Challenges are to be overcome and help me learn and grow.

   B. I don't like challenges.

6. **A.** If something is difficult, I want to give up.

   B. If something is difficult, I keep trying.

7. **A.** If someone succeeds, that inspires me to do the same.

   B. If someone else succeeds, I feel threatened and jealous.

Results:

1. A = 0, B = 1 – Intelligence
2. A = 0, B = 1 – Success
3. A = 1, B = 0 – Failure
4. A = 0, B = 1 – Feedback
5. A = 1, B = 0 – Challenges
6. A = 0, B = 1 – Difficulty
7. A = 1, B = 0 – Inspiration or intimidation

How did you do? Do you have more of a fixed or growth mindset?

If you got **7/7**, then you have 100% growth mindset!

5-6/7: mostly growth mindset with just 1 or 2 areas to work on. Make a note of these.

3-4/7: you have a mixed balance of growth and fixed. Again, make a note of the fixed areas that you need to work on.

0-2/7: you have mostly a fixed mindset. Take note of the fixed mindset areas that need work.

0 is 100% fixed mindset. Lots of learning and developing to grow your state of mind.

Adapted from: Dweck, C. S. (2006). *Mindset: The new psychology of success.*

If you need to develop your growth state of mind based on the questions above, here are some ways that you can evolve your thinking:

1. Acknowledge your weaknesses. We all have them, and that's ok. Let's find out what they are and look at ways to work on them. Ask questions such as, "How can I…" Take note of your strengths, too. Whilst it's useful to acknowledge weaknesses so that you can work on these areas, knowing your strengths is important so that you can focus on them to get results.

2. View challenges and setbacks as an opportunity to grow. We all come across challenges in our lives and these challenges can help us grow. Try not to see them as obstacles and reasons to give up,

but a chance to learn, to overcome these challenges and develop new skills so that you can be better next time.

3. Try different learning strategies; what works for one person may not work for you. Find out what works best for you, learn and practise in that way.

4. Replace the word 'mistake' with the word 'learn'. Mistakes are opportunities to learn. When something doesn't go your way, this is a great opportunity to learn and grow so that you can be a better version of yourself going forward.

5. Set goals and have steps in place to achieve them. It's just as important to set goals as it is to have action steps to reach those goals.

6. Value the journey and the end result. Sometimes it's easy to focus on your end goal and believe that you will only be happy once you reach this goal. However, what you are doing here is delaying being happy until that time. You are missing out on the present, what is happening in your life right now and the enjoyment of the moment.

7. Celebrate growth with others. Take the time to celebrate your achievements and those of other people. It will help, inspire and motivate you all to move forward.

8. Embrace challenges, be resilient and use them as a way to learn. Life's challenges are great for us to grow, learn and find solutions

to problems. Become a problem solver and when you try something that doesn't work, that's an opportunity to learn, be resilient and try again.

9. Be inspired by the success of others and only compete to be a better version of yourself. When others succeed, we can be inspired by what they have done and use their example to motivate ourselves so that we can achieve the success we desire.

10. Persist in the face of setbacks. Sometimes life doesn't go our way and that's ok. When we face these challenges, it's how we respond to them that matters. To keep going and persist when we experience setbacks is so important to help us reach our goals.

11. Learn from criticism and see it as constructive feedback. Criticism isn't personal and if we listen to it, we can take that feedback and learn so that we can perform better going forward.

See effort as a journey to mastery. Often when someone is successful, we only see the success and not all the hard work and many hours that person has spent to achieve their success. We all have to put in time and effort to master tasks and reach our goals.

CHAPTER FOUR

THE STATE OF MIND PRINCIPLES BLUEPRINT

Let's start by firstly introducing the principles that make up the state of mind blueprint.

Remember, you can learn all ten principles in this book so that you can take action and be successful in your business. I am a sportsperson, and I have applied this state of mind to my property business to be successful. By transferring the state of mind skills I have learnt and researched from sport into property entrepreneurship, I have been able to use this knowledge and experience to create the state of mind principles blueprint to help you do the same. The great news is that this blueprint can be learnt by anyone, and you can apply these principles in a way that works for you.

I learnt these principles from participating in sport at a high level, so I was developing the state of mind needed to achieve my success as a child.

Not everyone I started with or trained with as a figure skater progressed to be a high-level performer or achieved their version of success. Many dropped out, for example, when faced with challenges at different levels. The same is true in business and property. How many times do you see people give up too soon when starting or scaling a business?

From detailed research of the successful and elite figure skaters that I was surrounded by, I noticed that these athletes had developed a state of mind that had certain qualities that made them successful. They all had similar traits or what I have termed now to be principles. There was a small minority at this level that 'kept on going.' The interesting point to note here is that these individuals were not necessarily the most talented, but they had learnt a state of mind from sport that kept them on the ice and progressing to keep on achieving, despite any setbacks.

Whilst you too can learn these principles and do the same, not everyone will. Why is that? It isn't circumstance, as the people who do achieve often don't have circumstances that provide them with an unfair advantage over anyone else in the same situation. So, what is it that differentiates these people? Although many people have all the knowledge they require, say they would love to start a business, be an entrepreneur or invest in property, there are so many people who have been unable to fully focus on growing their business or, when investing, expanding their portfolio.

Learning the state of mind principles isn't enough; you need to develop these principles over time by being open to a growth state of mind, as discussed in the previous chapter, then use the principles and exercises in this book to take action. Often fear plays a very important part; the fear of failure stops us from taking action. However, being open to developing a growth state of mind and putting the principles into practice will guide you to overcome your fears and take the all-important action.

Are you ready to grow? Read on.

1. Desire, Reason Why

This is the starting point that underpins our business journey, having a strong desire and reason why drives us to achieve success even in difficult times. Having a desire is the state of mind where you have a longing for something, and you are so excited that you want to take action towards that something—your TOP goal or purpose. "The primitive sign of wanting is trying to get." (Anscombe 2000.)

Your ultimate reason why is the cause that moves you towards your goal. You need to be clear on this and know your reason why to keep you going. Why do you want to be a business owner or entrepreneur?

2. Goal-Oriented

Being goal-oriented is being focused on achieving the desired result. As a sportsperson, I set goals for everything, and I update them regularly. For me, it is one of the most important tasks I do. How do you achieve something when you don't know what it is you are trying to achieve? Athletes are usually goal-oriented, both short and long term, setting personal and team goals for team sports. They then train every day to reach their goals and push through their boundaries. As a young athlete, I always looked to get out of my comfort zone and be that bit better than I was the day before. Sportspeople also proactively reach out to get tools and techniques that will help them perform better. The same is true in the business world. Goals are crucial for success as they give us a stake in the ground, a destination for us to reach, and we can monitor our progress towards this worthwhile destination. A business needs goals so that you have direction and can operate effectively. Without goals, we are unable to track and monitor our performance levels and measure progress.

3. Routine

Since I was seven, I have had a routine in my life. To ensure that I could skate, be at school, do my homework, and take ballet classes, a plan and routine needed to be in place. I grew up with this and therefore applied the same structure to my business and my life in general. As a sportsperson, I've always got up early in the morning to exercise, and the same is true now. In this principle, I will show you how you can have your own routine in your business so that you get results.

4. Celebrate Success and Learn from Mistakes

It's well known that athletes are capable of handling and managing failure well, which is imperative in the entrepreneurial world. Learning from failure gives us a mental toughness. Sportspeople realise that these failures will give them an opportunity to learn, overcoming challenges and defeats. This is the same as being an entrepreneur. An entrepreneur faces many roadblocks. They also learn how to cope with failure and use the learnings to be better and succeed.

At the same time, athletes know when to celebrate the results they achieve, take credit for how far they have come and give themselves praise for a job well done. This is the same in business, we need to ensure that we celebrate the success we achieve. Every negotiation with an agent in the property business, meeting with a builder, or investor presentation is a valuable experience. You may not get the right deal, renovation completed, or investment required first time, but you can learn from it and do better next time.

Real entrepreneurs hold themselves accountable for their mistakes and weaknesses.

5. **Persistence and Resilience**

Sportspeople do not give up and will keep going despite any setbacks they may face. It's important, of course, to work out what went wrong, take the learnings and make the necessary changes to try again next time. Taking this mentality into the business and entrepreneurial world is incredibly worthwhile, especially at the start, as there will be many barriers and many 'no's' before hearing one 'yes'. Whether trying to get investment for your business, joint venture partners or finding suppliers, you need to be persistent and ensure you keep going until you succeed or get the answer you want.

Going hand in hand with persistence is resilience. It's a part of life that we all experience failure or, in fact, opportunities to learn. This happens a lot as an athlete. In training sessions, over weeks and sometimes months, I would execute the same move several times before making the change that would mean a successful execution. However, I would need to go through this learning process to find out what worked, literally falling down and getting back up. The same would happen in competitions, some performances were good and some not so good. This is the same for business and entrepreneurship. It's all about learning from things that did not go well, brushing them off or getting back up, and then to keep on going.

6. **Positive Attitude... With an Element of Realism**

At times, life doesn't always go to plan, but it's how we deal with life's challenges that make the difference. Sportspeople manage their emotions and entrepreneurs need to do the same. This does not mean being positive all the time. However, to move on in a positive way, we need to deal with our emotions first so that we have the right state of mind to find solutions to our problems. Entrepreneurs are problem solvers, and we need to be in the right state of mind to do this.

7. **Confidence**

For me, this is right at the top of the quality list. Without self-belief or confidence, an athlete just won't perform to the best of their ability. Self-belief is required so that a sportsperson will take informed risks, make decisions and take actions to get the results that they desire. Having confidence as an entrepreneur is the same. Confidence in yourself and your abilities makes a BIG difference to what you will achieve in your business. We will also explore your confidence in money—your money state of mind—as how you manage, feel and think about money is crucial when running a successful business.

8. **It's Not Easy But It Is Doable**

Participating in a competitive sport is not easy, but it is doable, and the same is true for being a business owner or entrepreneur. If sport, property investing or running a business was easy, then everyone would do it and succeed. It's not easy, but it's not rocket science either. Many people invest in property, start businesses and take action, but you need to accept that it is not going to be easy. There will be some bumps in the road along the way, but it is possible to be successful, especially with the powerful tools and techniques I'm sharing with you in this book.

9. Motivation

Professional sportspeople, high performers and Olympic athletes are often self-driven and rarely need extra motivation to get things done. Athletes constantly push themselves each day to work out, eat right and maintain their fitness, even on tough days. These days are more difficult for sportspeople and entrepreneurs to focus and put in the effort, but what makes a difference is that when it counts, a sportsperson will motivate themselves to get the job done. This motivation can be applied directly to entrepreneurship to get results.

10. Determination and Grit

Determination and grit are elements of mental toughness. The ability to mentally and psychologically be under pressure and still perform at peak efficiency. I believe this to be one of the most important qualities both a sportsperson and an entrepreneur must have, as only the mentally tough survive the journey. Both grit and determination help to consistently practise, get through hard training sessions, and be mentally ready to perform in competitions. Athletes test their physical and mental capability and limits every day. This mental toughness means that they can persist when rejected and remain calm under pressure if their training or competitions don't go to plan. To succeed in business, the same level of determination and grit is required. Rejections and challenges are part of sport, property, business and life.

11. Sacrifice

This is a bonus to the ten principles, and is last, but by no means least. Making a sacrifice is to choose to give up other things, that you may enjoy and value, for the sake of more important considerations that will get you closer to where you want to be. To realise your vision, desires and goals. If you want to succeed, there are some sacrifices you will need to make to achieve your goals. It's like wanting to be fit, healthy and slim; you'll need to sacrifice not all but most chocolate bars. As a sportsperson, I would need to give up time with friends at parties or watching TV to practise. An example in property would be prioritising appreciating assets over depreciating assets, that is, houses instead of fast cars!

The principles above are interwoven, having both crossovers and interdependencies. To learn and practise each principle effectively, you should follow the book in the order provided and practise all the exercises as you finish reading each chapter to build your state of mind.

Starting at the beginning… what fuels us?

First, you need a strong desire to succeed, a reason that will make you want to set goals, have something to be determined and motivated about. So this is where we are going to start our journey to develop the state of mind principles. As you grow your state of mind in one principle, you will see an improvement in the other principles.

Let's start with Principle One…

CHAPTER FIVE

PRINCIPLE #1: DESIRE AND REASON WHY

Having a desire with a clear reason why is a great starting point for your journey. This will fuel your actions to be successful in business. It is so important to know why you want to be a business owner or entrepreneur before you start, as this will drive you every day to keep going and keep you focused on your journey.

Before we get started, let's first consider the definitions of desire and reason so that we fully understand what these terms mean. I will begin every chapter in this way so that you have a clear understanding of each of the principles within this book to help you learn them in the best way possible.

> ## Definition
>
> **Desire:** a strong feeling of wanting to have something or wishing for something to happen.

> ## Definition
>
> **Reason (why):** a basis or cause, as for some belief, action, fact, event, etc. Explanation or justification.

This means we require a strong feeling to want something and a cause that we believe in to achieve what we want to do, for example, a TOP goal in life. So, the next question is, what do we define as being a TOP goal?

A TOP goal is the object of a person's ambition or effort; an aim or desired result. For example, 'She achieved her goal of becoming a British champion tennis player.' This is a future desired result that is part of our vision.

Whether you are an aspiring top athlete, singer, actor, entrepreneur or property investor, a strong desire and reason why is a key part of the ability to achieve success. If your need is strong enough, you will find a way to change your circumstances. However, the complete reverse is also true; if you are comfortable in life with a well-paid job, it can be challenging to create a strong desire to get out of your comfort zone and take action.

Those who have reached a professional level in sport or have successfully built a sizeable business, have created a strong desire or reason to get success. This may have come from the need to urgently generate enough money to live daily, from hating their 9-5 job or a strong desire to have a lavish lifestyle with a fancy car. Whatever their desire, it is an intense desire, and they all have a hunger to succeed.

Tip #1: Create a strong desire.

The first step and what I would consider the most important step in mapping out a route to your successful business outcome, is determining what will fuel your desire. You must clearly visualise and describe what being successful looks like for you, what is your reason, why are you doing this and not let go of that vision. The stronger your emotional connection is to your vision, the greater your chances are that you will achieve it.

Let's think of some examples.

If you decide to invest in property, you may do so because you would like to be financially independent. Perhaps you would like a pension plan, something to pass on to your children, it could be a lifestyle choice so that you don't have to work 9-5 and can spend more time with your family.

Another more personal example could be that you decide to follow an exercise programme because you want to lose weight, run a 5k, get into some skinny jeans, or perhaps you would like to run a marathon to raise money for a charity that's close to your heart.

As you can see from the examples above, you need to know why you show up every day, even if you don't feel like it.

Whether I was aiming for a championship medal or wanting lifestyle choices and financial independence from property, I knew my reason and therefore had that strong desire to achieve it. For property investing, I wanted lifestyle choices, the chance to make a difference, help others, and I had a vision of what my life would be like with financial independence. There are many reasons that you might want to be an entrepreneur, for example, passing on wealth to children, a pension or financial security. There are many others, I'm sure, as these are just some of the benefits that owning a business can give you; however, you will need to know why you want to take on a business venture and if this is a business that is also a lifestyle choice that you will enjoy.

Tip #2: You need a reason why.

The life we lead day in and day out is very significant. An essential part of my life is 'do what you love, love what you do.' You'll have a stronger desire to achieve, get motivated, be determined and be in flow with tasks if you enjoy what you do. Of course, there are always some aspects of what we do every day that we don't like. That is life and very natural. However, in the most part, we want to enjoy what we do. If I were to apply some logic to enjoying what you do each day, then I would say around 80% of what you do needs to be enjoyable, especially if this is a business to replace your job. That's what I have found to be the right level, but the idea is that you want to be spending the majority of your time out of your 9-5 job doing something that you enjoy and care about, rather than just replacing your job with something else you don't like.

Figure skating was always something I loved and was passionate about. As well as wanting to succeed and win, I enjoyed trying to master different tasks, like jumps, spins, steps, and be better each day at what I did. There was always a hunger to try to achieve, win and master a task that was enjoyable. We will discuss this later in Chapter 6: Principle #2: Goal-Oriented, but the point in this chapter is that I really enjoyed my practice sessions mastering tasks most of the time.

Tip #3: Do what you love, love what you do.

What is desire?

Let's take a more in-depth look at desire for a moment. Is it enough to want something bad enough, or is there more to desire than this? Having a strong desire is important, but this alone is not enough. The answer is there is more to desire than this. An athlete can really want to achieve a TOP goal but still not be motivated to take the complex steps needed to achieve it. Whilst it is vital to have a strong desire to achieve a goal, there also needs to be a strong desire to make the effort necessary. That is, to put the work in to fulfil that goal. In fact, we can classify these points into three levels of desire required to motivate us, and we need all of these levels to be successful.

The levels of desire are:
1. A strong desire to achieve a goal. This is the spark that starts the fire.
2. The strong desire to make the effort. To ensure the fire will keep burning. This is a desire and willingness to push on and not just keep going. This is a commitment and discipline that elite athletes

demand of themselves to make a continued focused effort constantly.

3.   A worthy TOP goal that the athlete is working to complete.

Athletes believe that they have the 'know-how' to achieve their goals, and they have the ability to fulfil them. If they don't believe this, then their motivation levels will fall, and they will not achieve their goal. They believe in themselves and their ability to carry out what has to be done successfully.

TOP Goals

So, this leads us on to goals. TOP goals! This is about having a strong desire and motivation to achieve a goal. Here are some examples of TOP goals:

'I want to win.'

'I want to be wealthy.'

'I want to be financially independent.'

So, what does this mean for you? What is your TOP goal? Why do you want to be a business owner or entrepreneur?

Take some time to think, and then go to the exercise section and write in your TOP goal. Ensure you have looked closely enough and have been very honest with yourself; after all, your TOP goal is what fuels your actions and propels you through life.

From speaking with professional athletes, and entrepreneurs, and from my own experience, there are often different levels of meaning with 'TOP goals' that we should fully explore so that we really understand what they mean to us. Here is an example of one of my TOP goals:

1. **Question:** What is your TOP goal?

    Answer: To be the best I can be, to be my version of successful and help others do the same.

2. **Question:** If you are at your best, you and others are successful, what will that mean?

    Answer: Enjoying life, financial independence, living life on my terms and helping other people to live life on their terms according to their values.

3. **Question:** What does enjoying life and living life on your terms look like?

    Answer: To have lifestyle choices and see others benefit from achieving this themselves.

TOP goal: to be the best version of myself. Financially independent to have lifestyle choices, living life on my terms, and help others do the same.

I believe we see these TOP goals as ways to feel complete; they allow us to realise the potential we have hidden inside of us. A feeling of hunger to keep going and push on, especially during tough times.

Take some time now to go to the exercises section in this chapter to complete the three questions above for yourself.

In sport, the TOP goal is the athlete's prime source of motivation, and this is crucial in my world of property investing and, of course, entrepreneurship. TOP goals are fundamental needs, part of philosophies to fulfil and make us whole. These essential needs give us a strong desire to fulfil them and sometimes a strong fear not to fulfil them. A combination of desire and fear often brings passion and intensity to an athlete's actions and the same can be true for an entrepreneur. These TOP goals are what really matter; they are essential and what we are striving for. An athlete who has a strong desire to demonstrate ability and a strong desire not to fail; their state of mind of striving can lead to very positive outcomes.

Why Desire and Reason Why are Important

At elite and professional levels, a strong desire to win is often the likely source of motivation for attaining optimal performance. However, this can sometimes be the desire to master a skill to a level of excellence, or to be the best that you can be. Either way, this want, desire and reason why ensures that you get up in the morning and it makes you committed to the process, so that you put in the effort to succeed. If you don't know what drives you and why you are doing something, you will find it difficult to overcome challenges when things get tough and to motivate yourself to carry on. Try the exercises at the end of this chapter to help you understand your reason why, so that you can get the desire and motivation to achieve your TOP goal.

Closing Quotes

—————

"Burning desire to be or do something gives us staying power—a reason to get up every morning or to pick ourselves up and start again after a disappointment."

Marsha Sinetar

—————

I also couldn't resist an amazing quote from Napoleon Hill, author of 'Think and Grow Rich', a book about 'success' and successful people:

"The starting point of all achievement is desire."

Exercises: Principle #1

Exercise #1 — TOP Goals Part One

Getting motivated comes down to asking yourself about your TOP goals. This is a really important step, so take the time to think about these questions. If possible, in a quiet room where you won't be disturbed or go out walking and find a quiet spot. Sometimes being out in nature can be an inspiration. I found this when we got our beautiful Labrador Lucca. I use my dog walks as 'thinking time' to think through solutions to challenges and ask some of the questions below.

What is really important to you?

_____

_____

_____

_____

_____

What are your most important values?

_____

_____

_____

_____

_____

What drives you?

_____

_____

_____

_____

_____

Exercise #2 — TOP Goals Part Two

1. What is your TOP goal?

    _____

    _____

2. If you [answer for question 1], what will that mean?

    _____

    _____

    If you _____,what will that mean?

    _____

    _____

    _____

3. What does [answer for question 2] look like?

    _____

    _____

    _____

    What does _____look like?

    _____

    _____

    _____

Exercise #3 — Business TOP Goals

Here are some business-related questions to answer:

What is the reason why you would like to start a business or be an entrepreneur?

_____

_____

_____

_____

_____

What problems would you solve or who would you help in your business?

_____

_____

_____

_____

_____

What would you do with your time if you didn't work 9-5?

_____

_____

_____

_____

_____

What do you enjoy?

_____

_____

_____

_____

_____

Will you enjoy this business?

_____

_____

_____

_____

_____

Vision Board

Let's create a vision board for your life around your TOP goal and what your business journey will help you create. This is a fun and very powerful exercise that can help you visualise what you would like in your life, your values and what you would like to achieve. Putting your vision board where you can see it every day also helps your subconscious start working on the solutions and trying to get you closer to what is on your board. Firstly, let's really explore what a vision board is:

A vision board is a visualisation tool that refers to a board of any kind, that can be used to make a collage of photos and words that represent your goals and dreams. They can be bought from a professional supplier or made by purchasing the products separately.

Firstly, you'll need to set aside 2-3 hours to complete your board.

Vision board kit: a canvas (11x14 is ideal), easel, acrylic paint, plastic table cover, paintbrush, decoupage glue, scissors, paint palette, two disposable cups, water, a hairdryer, stirrer, wipes or paper towel, marker pens and a paint knife.

You'll also need the following: magazines, access to a computer, internet, printer and paper, old cards, newspapers.

Ensure you protect your floor, furnishings and of course yourself: tablecloth, waist bin, apron, gloves if needed.

Cleaning items: paper towels and wipes.

Seven Steps to Create Your Vision Board:

1. Think about different areas of your life, for example, a car, house, charity, travel, lifestyle, family, health, business, fitness, challenges, values, happiness and any photos that inspire, motivate, bring joy or mean something to you.

2. Use magazines, the internet, newspapers, etc., to find photos or words, i.e., if you'd like a Porsche, then find a picture of that car, model and desired colour. Try to be specific as you can. What are your values? Find quotes or write down a sentence that means something to you. What motivates you? If there is a place you would like to visit, then find a picture of that place. Ideal house, inside and outside, find some pictures/words. Then it's time to cut them out so you are ready to add them to your vision board. Take some time to free your mind as much as you can and if you are looking for words or a phrase that you can't find, then write it down with a marker pen. Try not to limit yourself and imagine that you a kid in a sweet shop and can pick anything you want. Make sure you write out your TOP goal as in the previous exercise, so you can add this to your board.

3. Decorate your canvas. What's your favourite colour? Use the palette and acrylics to mix colours if needed. Mix them using the stirrer. If you have two, then, of course, add two halves to your pages with these colours. If you have more, go ahead and add more, by dividing the board up further. It's your vision board, after all! Note that the more water you use, the more watercolour effect you will have; less water will create a denser colour. Use two cups of water, one for dirty and one for clean, and a paper towel to blot dry. It's useful to speed up the paint drying process by using a hairdryer.

4. Colour mixes: yellow + red = orange, yellow + blue = green, blue + red = purple.

5. Now it's time to design your board! Arrange your photos and cut outs on the dry canvas (make sure it's dry). Once you have everything in place, then take a photo. Move all cut outs off the board and place them on the table close by. Discard any cuttings in the waste bin, so you don't glue anything to your board by mistake.

6. Time to glue everything in place. Have your photos to hand from the previous step. Add some glue to a cup and a little water, then mix well with a stirrer. Dip the brush in the glue, ready to go. Work left to right, top to bottom and start by brushing some glue on the canvas in small sections, sticking your cut outs one at a time to the board. Smooth them out to avoid any wrinkles. Use the wipes to remove any excess glue. (Note, the decoupage glue dries clear.)

7. Start from the centre outwards and apply glue over all cut outs; use a brush to smooth out wrinkles. Then apply the glue to the entire canvas.

8. Your vision board is finished!

Congratulations! You've taken a very positive and proactive step in your life. A vision board is the first step of the journey to planning out your life road map and will give you the strength, confidence and encouragement you need to take action towards your goals; giving you both the desire and motivation to go after what really matters to you in your life.

CHAPTER SIX

———

PRINCIPLE #2: GOAL-ORIENTED

In a nutshell, people with a goal-oriented state of mind plan out what they would like to achieve and then work on the tasks that will help them attain their desired outcome. In sport, being goal-focused is essential to achieving success and applied to business, having task-oriented goals with routine enables you to take action to start. We will take some time to understand more about what goals are, how you can become goal-oriented, the importance of goals, and enjoying the journey. By the end of this chapter, you should have 'SMART' goals for your business and some action steps to get there.

> ## Definition
>
> **Goal:** the object of a person's ambition or effort; an aim or desired result.

Definition

Goal-Oriented: being focused on reaching a specific objective, or accomplishing a given set of tasks 'concerned with or focused on achieving a particular aim or desired result.'

How Do You Become a Goal-Oriented Person?

Being a goal-oriented individual can produce impactful results as an entrepreneur. Whether you are starting a business, are new to investing or an experienced business owner, it is so important to learn the process of goal setting, tracking and reviewing progress against goals and adjusting your strategy as required. We will explore below how you can develop a goal-oriented state of mind to help you achieve success.

Sportspeople are usually goal-oriented or focus on task-oriented goals to get the results they want to be successful. However, the tasks and the process are one of the most important aspects of working towards a goal. Whilst it is essential to have a worthwhile TOP goal, it is equally important that this goal is defined correctly and broken down into achievable goals, subgoals and tasks or actions. This should be followed up with plans, processes and routines to achieve the goal.

Although some people don't set goals or fear goals, many do set them and don't always achieve them. There can be several reasons for this, but one of the most common reasons is not clearly defining them with steps, tasks and actions to get to the end goal. Another reason, covered in the Chapter Seven, Principle #3: Routine, is not having a plan or process in place. This is like saying, "I'm going to New York" without setting the tasks and actions, such as booking your flight, your hotel and planning your trip.

Unless you take the appropriate steps, master set tasks, put plans in place and take action towards a goal, it just won't happen. Relating this to business means that you must do something to make your journey as an entrepreneur actually happen.

Being goal-oriented is about completing relevant tasks in a set order to get the desired result. To complete and master these tasks, you need to be task-driven or task-oriented to achieve your goal. Someone who is goal-oriented uses tasks, targets and results to stay motivated to achieve their long-term goal.

In this chapter, we will focus our attention on the first part of setting goals and mapping out the steps and actions to achieve these goals. As mentioned above, routine will help create processes around the goals you set.

Task-Oriented Goals

Task-oriented means being focused on completing specific tasks that will help achieve the success of your TOP goal. I believe it is fair to say that a series of successfully completed tasks achieve goals; therefore, we will be drawing attention to task-oriented goals. In sport, athletes focus on setting their goals and then focusing on mastering specific tasks or skills to get their results. By mastering a particular move in sport, an athlete gains competence in their ability that leads to motivation, through measuring success and overall improvement towards their goal. In property, this may be mastering the negotiation skills with agents to ensure that you get the best deal. In business, this may be getting your pitch just right to get the investment required for your business, or mastering your sales script to drive the sales within your business. This will take some practise to refine, but practising will lead to task mastery.

What is the Importance of Being Goal-Oriented?

Goal-oriented people will set targets with specific objectives and master the tasks to progress towards their goal; they will often put in any extra work required whenever there is a competition or a particular deadline to be met.

As a sportsperson and professional coach, I have always had goal setting as part of my life and, as such, I have become a goal-oriented individual. At the start of a season, competitions, tests and personal achievements would be set out on a timeline as SMART (Specific, Measurable, Achievable, Realistic, Timely) goals with a training plan of how those goals would be achieved. I didn't really know they were SMART at the time; however, the important point here is that it was not just about the overall goals for the season, but equally important was the route to getting there. That is, the training plan, routine, and process needed to ensure these goals could be met.

Focusing both on tasks to fulfil goals and the goals themselves creates an ideal balance. Goals come from our TOP goal, desire, reasons why and our vision board. You set these goals to achieve your vision. However, you need to enjoy what you do, and the vision board sets out what you are interested in and love doing, which should fuel some of the tasks you will be doing every day. Goals and tasks you enjoy work together with focused routines, processes and planning. There's a lot of merit in setting clear goals to aim for with tasks and a process to follow, as well as the focused practice of a specific task to be mastered to fulfil a goal.

Goal Setting — SMART Goals

To start, it's worth considering goal setting first as this helps to focus attention and is very important to maintain and enhance motivation.

SMART goal setting sets a direction for both the short term and long term. Goals should be divided into smaller sub-goals with tasks to complete so that it's possible to have manageable 'chunks' of the overall goal to work on. Seeing the success achieved in the short term will maintain motivation.

Being motivated is key for success in sport, and the same is also true for entrepreneurship. Motivation is a principle we will cover later in the book, but first, we need goals and tasks to get motivated about, related to our vision and reason why. Understanding what drives our goals—as shown in the exercises completed in the previous chapter—improves how and why athletes train the way they do.

I have found, during many years as a professional sports coach, that athletes are all different as individuals and motivated by different goals and tasks. Goals are crucial to measure how well an athlete is progressing, but there is also a need to focus specifically on the skills to be mastered to achieve these goals that will need practising in training sessions. Sometimes, as an athlete, I preferred to take a purely task-oriented approach, so I could focus purely on one task at a time when training. This is true for many sportspeople that I trained with, and this approach often puts an athlete in flow and enjoyment—something we all want to achieve when working on our business. Being in flow is an excellent experience; when we are fully submerged in a task, we don't notice the world around us. These tasks are like bricks that form part of a house, and they need to be carefully laid one at a time for the house to become complete. Setting goals and then learning to master and complete tasks (laying the bricks) will lead you to your goal (the built house).

Here are three examples to consider for sport and entrepreneurship:

1. If you're a figure skater, your goal might be to win a regional championship. The steps to make progress towards this goal may

be to get a coach that will help you attain the level required, then together, you would put a training plan in place to get there. You would perhaps need to select a personal trainer to get off-ice exercise sessions planned and book in a choreographer to get programmes in place.

2. If you're starting a property investing business, your goal might be to own a million-pound property portfolio. Therefore, you would need to put steps and actions in place to get knowledge of how to invest in property, where to invest, what your market is and then to write a property business plan.

3. If you are starting in business, your goal might be to own a business that has profits of £100,000 every year. Some of the actions and steps to put in place to start could be to join some business start-up groups, test your business idea, get knowledge of how to start a business, get feedback about your business niche, and to research and write a business plan.

The goal in sport is to perform to your best and win; however, in figure skating, for example, you would not spend all your time focusing on your marks to try to be better or get a higher score. To be successful requires focusing on disciplined practice to get better each day, combined with goal setting. That is what will help you to win a competition. If you want results, then it's worth focusing your attention on both setting task-oriented goals and putting plans, processes, and routines in place to attain your goals. So how do we make sure that we focus on what we might call 'the journey' towards our worthy goal? Basically, we need to enjoy and be immersed in the journey itself.

Enjoy the Journey

When setting goals, it's easy to think that you'll be happy when you reach the goal. However, you need to be present to enjoy each step on the way to attaining your business goals. Otherwise, you will only associate the feeling of being happy with reaching a goal, meaning, for example, you will only be satisfied when you have achieved a million-pound business. However, there is a lot of fun to be had in enjoying what we do and experiencing flow in the tasks we are doing every day. There will, of course, be tasks we don't like, and there will also be setbacks on the way, but overall, we should be enjoying the process to achieve our goal and not just focusing on the end destination to be happy. We will learn how to tackle setbacks and challenges later in the book.

Updating and Replacing Goals

With a goal-oriented state of mind, we do need to replace a goal once we've achieved it so that we can keep moving forward. What do you do next? Well, you can set a new goal that aligns with your TOP goal, vision board or a new chapter in life. Perhaps you'll need a new vision board too?

I believe that life shouldn't be about any single accomplishment; it's a set of goals that we achieve, develop and evolve all the time. Goals don't have to be fixed, not even your TOP goal; they can be updated at any time, and in fact, I think it is important we do, as we change and grow all the time. Therefore, we should be updating our goals, modifying, reviewing them and replacing a goal if we achieve it. It is about progression, achievement, refinement of tasks, pivoting and continuous improvement. It is your commitment to your goals and the tasks, routines and processes that will determine your progress.

Learning to Love Routines, Plans and Processes

Tip #4: Goals are great for planning your progress. Have process steps in place to help you move forward.

Goals can provide direction and even push you forward, so it is essential to set these first. However, you will need well-designed plans, routines and processes of how to get there. Routines, covered in the next chapter, will give you plans with a time and a place to help you work on the tasks required to reach your goals. This matters as committing to both will mean you will take action that will really make the difference to what you achieve.

In this chapter, the exercises will focus purely on first learning how to set your SMART goals for your business, explaining what they are, looking at your options to achieve them and setting tasks to take action to achieve your goals. This will help to make you a more goal-oriented person.

Remember:

It is good to challenge yourself so that you are in control of the situation and keep focused on the desired outcome. When striving to achieve a goal that has been set, it's also important not to lose sight of your TOP goal, desired outcome and your vision. Remember to be faithful to your goals, never give up and keep focused until the end.

Remember that successful people do not give up and keep finding new ways to meet their goals. To be successful in achieving your goal, you need to take action on the task at hand and not procrastinate at the start or during the process. Self-discipline is essential to goal attainment and making you a successful entrepreneur.

Tip #5: Remember not to lose sight of your vision and TOP goal.

It's also important to understand that any failures in specific tasks do not mean that you won't achieve the goal. In fact, this gives you an opportunity to learn and to repeat tasks in the process so that you can refine them to achieve your goal.

Example of Goal Setting

Let's consider an example of setting goals in property investing:

In five years, I will own a property portfolio of £3 million with a yield per year of £147,600. I will be financially independent by the end of year two. I will need a 'power team' of plumber, builder, electrician, solicitor, and mortgage broker to achieve this goal.

Year One, Year Three and Year Five

Year One: portfolio profit per year of £10,800, owning two Buy To Let (BTL) houses. Portfolio Value: £600k

Year Three: portfolio profit per year of £57,600, owning two house shares, and four BTL. Portfolio Value: £1.8million

Year Five: profit from portfolio per year of £147,600, owning five house shares, four BTL and one serviced accommodation. Portfolio Value: £3 million

This is based on the average house share profit I have achieved per month, the average Buy To Let profit per month and average for serviced accommodation. As these are averages, they may sometimes be slightly higher or lower depending on the house location and size, etc.

These will need to be divided further into quarterly and monthly subgoals.

Closing Quote

In the words of Albert Einstein, "If you want to live a happy life, tie it to a goal, not to people or things."

Exercises: Principle #2

Locke and Latham (1990) have a goal-setting theory of motivation that states if goal commitment is both specific and challenging, then it leads to higher task performance than a goal that is not clearly defined. Over 500 empirical studies support this theory. (Latham, Locke, & Fassina, 2002; Locke & Latham, 2002)

Goal-oriented people practise a variety of skills that allow them to set realistic goals, challenge simple objectives and track their progress. We will be focusing on goals, tasks and the process as a complete goal achieving system in these exercises.

Follow the methods below to help you set SMART goals and be a more goal-oriented individual:

Exercise #1 - SMART Goals

- Start with the initial goal you have in mind.

_____

_____

_____

_____

_____

- **Specific** – what do you want to accomplish? Who is involved?

_____

_____

_____

_____

_____

- **Measurable** – how can you measure progress? How do you know you've been successful?

_____

_____

_____

_____

_____

- **Achievable** – do you have the skills required? If not, can you get them? What's the motivation?

_____

_____

_____

_____

_____

- **Realistic** – why are you setting this goal? Is this aligned with your business?

_____

_____

_____

_____

_____

- **Time** – realistic time to complete.

_____

_____

_____

_____

_____

Exercise #2 — Storyboard (Using Your SMART Goal)

Storyboarding enables you to access your creative (right) side of your brain whilst planning. This is an activity that is usually driven by your rational logical (left) brain. Our creative brain gets engaged as we draw, rather than write. Moving between present and future states opens up our imagination. We consider actions we might not have thought of and as we imagine ourselves taking action, we become much more likely to do so.

This exercise is designed as a warm up exercise to Exercise #3 to help you visualise getting from where you are now to where you want to be, so you can start planning your steps to get to your SMART goal.

- Take a piece of A4 paper and divide it into six boxes by folding it as shown.

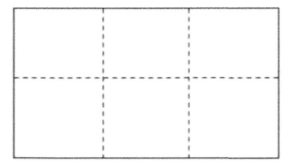

- Draw a line 1cm up from the bottom of each box
- In the top left box, draw an image of your current reality.
- In the bottom right box, draw an image of your goal or you achieving your goal.
- In the top middle box, draw an image of the first action you will take towards your goal.
- In the bottom middle box draw an image of what will happen just before you've achieved your goal.

- In the bottom left box, draw an image of what will happen just before what is happening in the bottom middle box

- In the top right box draw an image of the second action you will take towards your goal.

- Below the line in each box, write one word that represents what you are doing.

Exercise #3 - GROW

GROW is a coaching method that helps us get to our goals. GROW stands for Goal, Reality, Options, Will and basically plans the steps to reach a goal, arrange tasks in a logical order, explore your options, gather resources and set actions towards reaching your goal. Let's try using GROW for your SMART goal in Exercise #1.

- Your GOAL – enter the SMART goal from Exercise #1

_____

_____

_____

_____

_____

- Your REALITY – what is your starting point right now?

_____

_____

_____

_____

_____

- Your OPTIONS to achieve your goal – what could you do to achieve your goal? Be creative and think of as many options as you can.

_____

_____

_____

_____

_____

- What WILL you do? List the tasks you will undertake to achieve the goal and the actions you will take to accomplish the tasks:

Task: _____

_____

_____

_____

_____

Task: _____

_____

_____

_____

_____

Task: _____

_____

_____

_____

_____

Task: _____

_____

_____

_____

_____

When you've completed the exercise above, consider the following:

- Decisions about your tasks: there may be tasks that are more urgent or important, so look at your options, anticipate what the outcome may be, then decide the tasks to complete, the order you should complete them in, giving them a date and who should complete the task.

- Organise your actions by priority: firstly, your tasks become actions when you give them an owner and a deadline, so we will now refer to your tasks as actions. Note what actions you should complete first. Make sure you have a system set up that means you work on actions in order to meet your goals. You can do this by prioritising your actions based on complexity, urgency and priority—perhaps you might prefer to complete complex, time-intensive actions first. Assign a number in terms of priority to each action so you know what order to do them in to reach your goal.

- Time management: check the target date. Clear deadlines ensure you make progress on your goals. You can use scheduling or calendar management to assign yourself short-term milestones that lead to achieving long-term goals.

- Measurement of Success: how will you know when you've achieved this action? Knowing what the result of taking an action will be is key, otherwise how will you know when you've reached that point, completed the action and perhaps fulfilled or mastered the task?
- Are there any actions that are repetitive? Note down if these could be done by someone else (outsourced) or automated.

Action	Owner	Target Date	Priority	Measurement of Success

To download the playbook for goal setting, go to www.stateofmindplaybook.com.

Exercise #4: What Tasks are You Enjoying?

Being goal-oriented means prioritising and completing the tasks that will help get you closer to reaching your desired outcome. Next, we will explore how you can plan your time around your goals, review progress and set routines so that you work to achieve your goals, a necessity of being a goal-oriented person.

Note the tasks you are enjoying here:

_____

_____

_____

_____

_____

_____

CHAPTER SEVEN

———

PRINCIPLE #3: ROUTINE

Following on from the previous chapter that focused on task-oriented goal setting, this chapter gives you the next step: routine, plans, and processes to achieve your goals. We mentioned that these are key to achieving your goals as routines and plans are part of the steps and the actions you will take every day to get to where you want to be. As you develop and repeat your routines, they can turn into habits, meaning you'll be able to unconsciously take action towards your goals in a similar way to learning how to ride a bike or drive a car.

Firstly, let's understand more about what routines, habits, plans, and processes are so we can put these in place for your business.

What is a Routine?

> ## Definition
>
> **Routine:** a sequence of actions regularly followed.

When reading the definition of routine, I'm sure you will agree that habits come to mind? So, the question is, how is a routine different to a habit? Well, a habit can be defined as…

> ## Definition
>
> **Habit:** an action we often do in a regular and repeated way.

The definitions for routine and habit look the same, so what differentiates them? The difference is that a routine is a regular way of doing something in a specific order with both intentional thought and planning. However, a habit is recurrent without conscious thought that requires little to no planning or deliberate effort.

There has been some focus and attention on habits in recent years, but where do these habits come from? You may have a habit to go to the same cupboard each morning and get your box of cereal for breakfast. You would have started this habit by assigning the cereal to that cupboard and, day after day, returning to that cupboard to get the cereal to make your breakfast. You would have started with a routine whereby you would need to think about the plan for your morning, but this will become a habit as you will at some point be able to go to the cupboard unconsciously. If you decide to change the cupboard, what happens? I'm sure you would first go to the same cupboard initially because you will have forgotten that the box of cereal has moved. However, eventually after creating a new routine, this new routine will become a new habit. Therefore, creating good routines can lead us to good habits whereby some or all of these processes are automated.

As well as having good routines that lead to good habits, we can also have bad routines that can lead to bad habits, such as drug addiction or smoking. However, it is possible to replace these, but it does require intentional thought and planning. Therefore, following another routine can lead us to a different habit. Similar to the analogy above, moving an item in a cupboard to a new place will require intentional thought at the start. Yet, over time by repeating a planned, intentional routine day after day, this task will become a habit whereby we may unconsciously do some or all of the task without thinking.

If we can think about routines and design them for our individual use, there is potential for significant growth to make these routines a habit. However, it does and will take dedication and repetition many, many times over. In figure skating, this was often referred to as practise makes permanent. The idea that if you keep practising the same move, good or bad, it will make that technique permanent. Notice not perfect! Only purposeful and focused practice of repeating an element on the ice the right way can make it excellent and perhaps perfect.

Routines from Figure Skating to Property Investing

From training in figure skating as a child, I had daily and weekly routines, which have now become habits. I always had routines in place because it was an absolute necessity to fit everything into my life, and a plan or schedule was needed so that I could get to school, go to the ice-rink, and ensure my homework was completed every day. The result was that many of these routines became habits over time. I also transferred most of these habits into my property business without realising I was disciplined in this way, or understanding the state of mind skills I had learned through sport that have served me so well in my business.

An interesting point emerged around what I defined as early morning. Now, 7 a.m. in the office, I assume to most people would seem early? It would to me too. However, 7 a.m. on the ice-rink would be a lie-in. Why? The best time for high-level athletes to practise would be 5 a.m. or 6 a.m., when no one was around and focused practice could be done. By 7 a.m., there were too many other skaters on the ice. You were only considered a serious competitor in figure skating if you were on the ice at 5 or 6 a.m. As a figure skating coach, if one of my pupils did not want to commit to this time in the morning, I assumed they were not serious enough to be a competitive skater. There is a level of commitment required to being a high-performing athlete, and only some are willing to put in the additional effort to achieve this level. In your business, are you ready to get up in the morning excited, committed, focused and willing to do what is necessary to achieve your business goals? This will determine how serious you are about being successful in your business.

Getting up early in the morning has been a routine that has turned into a habit from childhood. My routine was usually figure skating before school, then school, ballet, perhaps more figure skating after school, homework or piano lessons. There was no time for watching TV, so interestingly enough, I do not have much time for TV now. This is something I don't consciously do. It just does not occur to me to switch the TV on at any point in the day. It's only through planning that I watch TV—a film perhaps on Saturday evening to relax. This is scheduled as part of a routine. Likewise, if you want to introduce routines into your business, you will need to make an effort to do so consciously. Planning your routines to start with until they become habits over time.

So how do you make a start to implement routines that work for you and your business? Here are my top ten ways to start implementing routines:

1. **Create a business plan**

   Firstly, create a business plan. Failing to plan is planning to fail! A business plan is so important; it's a blueprint of your business and a must-have for anyone starting out. What helps us when we write a business plan is that we really think about our business idea. We research it thoroughly; we understand how we will reach our goals, how much profit we can make, how much money is needed to be financially independent, who are our competitors, where it is best to set up shop or invest for our target market, and who will be our customers. All of these questions will need to be answered before starting your business.

   The most common phrase I hear from people about business plans is, 'I'm worried that I won't follow the plan'. Remember, a business plan is a plan and plans change, so it should be a living document. If circumstances change in your business, which is likely, then the plan can be updated to reflect these changes.

   You may think, what does a business plan have to do with routine? Well, it's a plan that provides you with goals and tasks to achieve those goals, that will form your routine. Like all tasks in your routine, the business plan also needs to be part of the routine. You'll need to update the business plan every six months, ideally as you evolve and your business moves on and changes.

To guide you on what you need to include in a business plan, go to exercise #4 or you can download the playbook at www.stateofmindplaybook.com.

2. **Get a 'power team'**

Who are the 'power team'? Well, this depends on your business, but these are the people that you would need to rely on to run your business. An example in property investing could be builders, plumbers, electricians, solicitors, architects, accountants, basically all the key people required to complete a property project.

In skating, a 'power team' might be a coach, personal trainer, dressmaker, skating boot supplier, psychologist and nutritionist. These were the people I could trust and rely upon to help me reach my goals. Perhaps there may be people you will need to change or add as your business grows; however, the important point to remember is that you cannot achieve everything you want alone. You will not have all the skills essential for this. I learnt from a young age that I needed support for my figure skating journey, and I have applied this to my property business journey. Entrepreneurs I know also outsource tasks to specialists where required, so they can focus on their business growth.

Once you find the key people you can trust, then these people become members of your 'power team'. They are part of the routine either day to day or part of the process that you would follow each time when taking on a new project. You may have heard the term 'cookie cutter' or 'rinse and repeat'. This is essentially finding the team that works well for you and then repeating with the same team in a set routine. Perhaps you will want to increase the size of your projects each time, but essentially you are planning projects in a routine that will be followed time and time again.

Tip #6: Get a 'power team'.

---

3. **Set a time and place in the diary for tasks and stick to it!**
Tasks need a time and place. This is not simply about writing out a 'to-do' list, but scheduling time in the diary to do actions. For example, in property, I set aside an hour to research properties that fit my criteria where I would like to buy. Remember to make the task specific and focused so that your time is spent purposefully.

Tip #7: Set time aside in the day to do tasks and stick to that time.

---

4. **Have a set routine each day focusing on tasks to achieve your goals**
Choose the tasks that 'make your boat go faster', these are tasks that you prioritise because they work directly towards growing your business, generating income and reaching your goals.

Going back to the previous chapter, being goal-oriented also means prioritising and completing the tasks that help you reach your desired outcome in business. As above, a calendar with tasks planned and reminders set will assist you in working on those tasks when required and keeping track of your progress.

5. **Select three key actions to complete each day**

   Having a certain number of actions to focus on each day can make your tasks more manageable and increase your chance of getting more done. My recommendation is to target three key tasks to complete in a day, ranked in order of priority and schedule these in the evening of the day before. You can put small actions like sending an email. If you have something important that you don't want to do or that is complicated, then I recommend actioning that task first in the day. You will feel so much better when that task is done, and you can move on to enjoying your day.

6. **Choose hours to suit your lifestyle and your business needs**

   Who decides that 9-5 is a working day? I understand that most of the world operates to these hours, so being available during these hours makes sense when working with others or meeting customer needs. However, for your business, decide hours to work that suit your business and your lifestyle. Finding the times that you are most productive would be a good indication of when you should work on tasks that produce the most value for your business.

7. **Start and end your day in the same way**

   This really helps you stay organised, focused on your business and positive. I plan the next day at the end of the day before, and in the morning, I will review that plan. I always end the day focusing on what has been achieved.

This routine has been taken from the ice. My coach would always ask me to start and end a practice session with an element I could perform really well, like a warmup and cool down. Starting on a positive and ending positively. We would also plan my next session at the end of a lesson.

Applying and adapting this principle to business, I've outlined the process for you below, to execute your warmup and cool down in the business day. I've started with the end of the day first. You will understand why I present the end of the day followed by the start of the day when you read further.

'Cool-down' – end each day with:
-    A positive review of the day and achievements.
-    A plan for the next day based on those tasks and actions that generate income and further your business.

'Warm-up' – at the start of each day, do the following:
-    A positive review of yesterday's achievements.
-    Review the plan made the day before and tweak if necessary.

At the end of each day, focus on the achievements. It's so easy to look back at what you didn't do rather than what you DID do, but to keep positive and to move forward, it's imperative to take note of what you achieved. Review all of what you got done for the day and then plan for the next day.

8.   **Plan in advance**
It makes sense to have yearly, quarterly, monthly, weekly and daily plans for your business that set out the various tasks required to achieve long-term goals and smaller subgoals. Ensure you follow

up daily and weekly, reviewing what was achieved and ensuring plans and deadlines are kept up to date for the week ahead. Then, use the same process to track progress at the end of each month, quarter and year, refining your strategy as required to fulfil your goals.

9. **Use your vision board**

Your vision board can improve your preparation strategy to show the scope of your TOP goal. Ensure that you put your vision board in a visible place that you look at every day, to be constantly reminded of what you want to achieve in your life and business.

Tip #8: Remind yourself every day of your vision by making your vision board visible.

---

10. **Track your progress**

Every week, take an hour at a specific time to evaluate your long-term and short-term goals and the next steps required to achieve them.

Create a routine to regularly review how efficiently and effectively you are completing tasks and how much progress you have made in reaching specific goals. It's possible to use tools, apps or create your own method for tracking how long you spend on a given task. You could also record the time you start and finish a task. Finally, note any possible distractions that affect how much time you are spending on income-generating tasks. Tracking progress can help you identify any time-consuming and repetitive tasks or potential barriers that limit your productivity. This allows you to start streamlining your workflow, enabling you to improve your ability to work on tasks that help you achieve your goals.

When you find yourself repeating the same tasks in a routine that are not income-generating, ensure that you capture these tasks, recording the workflow, as these tasks will need outsourcing later.

How to approach routines

We can probably all agree that it's easier to watch TV or eat a chocolate bar and to stay in our old routines, perhaps because they have become habits for us. This is where we need a state of mind routine kickstart to get us thinking about how our routines serve us and benefit us. Rather than approaching routines by thinking about a short-term gain, another approach could be focusing on the long-term benefits. What we can do is ask ourselves three questions to unlock the immediate gains that will come to mind initially and then look at what the longer-term outcome could be. The key is to listen to your answer for question three below to determine how you think about a routine.

For example:

Let's reframe a bad routine.

1. Do you feel great when drinking a bottle of wine? Probably yes.
2. What about after you've had a bottle of wine? Yes, perhaps during that evening.

3. How do you feel the following day? Now that may be a bit painful and repeating that routine or habit may be even more painful and bad for your health long term.

Let's reframe a good routine.

1. How do you feel when starting a complex task? Perhaps you don't want to do it and you are feeling anxious.

2. What about during the task? Uncomfortable, you may be out of your comfort zone.

3. How do you feel once the complex task is complete? I'm guessing much better, and you may feel accomplished ready for the next challenge.

Try re-framing your routines and use the exercises in this book to help you form successful routines and habits.

Closing Quotes

"The Secret of your future is hidden in your daily routine."

Mike Murdock

"Routine is everything! 'Winning is a habit, so is losing."

Ivo Dos Santos,

competed in judo for Australia in the 2012 Olympic Games

Exercises: Principle #3

All of the plans and routines suggested in this chapter and the following exercises will require thought and focused effort to start. However, with consideration of our definitions, the more you practise, the easier your routines will become. If you keep going, you will start to form successful habits that you will do unconsciously, helping to create a way of life that will help you achieve your desired outcomes.

Exercise #1: 'You've Got This' Journal

You can use a notepad, diary, or download the State Of Mind Playbook which has the electronic version of the 'You've Got This' journal template ready for you to complete: go to www.stateofmindplaybook.com.

Day: [date] _____

What did I achieve yesterday:

1. _____

_____

_____

_____

2. _____

_____

_____

_____

3. _____

_____

_____

_____

Tasks to complete today:

1. _____

_____

_____

_____

2. _____

_____

_____

_____

3. _____

_____

_____

_____

I am grateful for...

_____

_____

_____

_____

_____

I have achieved in my business journey today:

1. _____

_____

_____

_____

2. _____

_____

_____

_____

3. _____

_____

_____

_____

Finding time in our schedule to practice gratitude grounds us and forms a reminder of the positive things in our lives. When we are dismayed by small setbacks, we forget not only what makes life great, but also the opportunities available to us. Gratitude is an incredibly uncomplicated yet very powerful tool. Keep a gratitude journal to record a daily 'I am grateful for…' list. The items on a gratitude list can cover anything which is meaningful to you; the weather, family and loved ones or perhaps recent experiences that have changed your life for the better. At the same time, also record your achievements and set three tasks for the day that you must do to help you fulfil your goals or reasons why.

Exercise #2: The 'Power Hour' and Booking Time Out in Your Diary

Schedule in a power hour for:

1. Exercise
2. Reading
3. Relaxation, visualisation or meditation

You may need to get up an hour earlier to schedule this in but it is well worth it to start your day in the right way. Or find a time to fit in the power hour that works for you, so that you have your 'right' day. If you need to split it up, then go ahead. If that's a morning meditation and a lunchtime workout with gratitude before bed, then you design your time your way. The key thing is that you are taking care of your mind, body and soul for the day with a power hour, so you are fully prepared for your day where you can be the best version of yourself. If you do find the hour too much, please just book some time in for yourself, even if it is just 10 minutes to prioritise you.

After this:

*   Review your diary for the planned day that you created the day before
*   Ensure you follow your diary so that you focus on income-generating tasks
*   Block time out in your diary tomorrow for income-generating tasks.

You may wonder, how does the power hour help you in your business? Well, it is about taking care of YOU so that you are in the best state of mind to show up for your business, make the best decisions and get the most out of your day, every day. I do a power hour every morning, and it really does work to give clarity to my day, to be the best version of myself and have the right state of mind to be successful.

Exercise #3: Reframe

How do you feel just before

_____?

How do you feel during

_____?

How do you feel after

_____?

Exercise #4: Business Plan Guide

1. **Executive Summary**

   1.1. **Business name** (What the name says about your business and how it influences potential customers)

   1.2. **Mission Statement** (What does your business offer? Who does it help? What is the overall purpose of your product(s)/service(s)? – keep it brief!)

   1.3. **About the founders and business** (A bit about you and your background. How is your experience relevant?)

   1.4. **Service or product** (Describe your product(s) or service(s))

   1.5. **Financial Summary** (Forecast of profit and turnover for year 1 to year 3)

1.6. **Elevator Pitch** (Who are you? What do you do? What do you want? Your elevator pitch should clearly state what your business does, who it's for and why it's different)

1.7. **Start-up financing requirements** (What do you need to start your business? How much will this cost?)

2. **Company Description** (key details about your company, where you are located? What do you do? What will you look to achieve?)

3. **The Team** (Who is in your team?)

4. **Industry Outlook** (Look at size, growth and trends in your industry)

5. **Target Market**

   5.1. What problem is your ideal customer facing?

   5.2. Who are your ideal customer?

      5.2.1. By economic segment

      5.2.2. By location

      5.2.3. By age

   5.3. What prompts your ideal customer to buy?

6. **Market Research** (Online research, interviews, questionnaires, surveys, with key findings from research. What's happening in the business world that makes your product/service a must?)

7. **Competitive Analysis and Unique Selling Point (**Who offers this product/service? What do they offer? Pros and Cons? How are you different?)

8. **Product(s)/Service(s) Description** (Describe the product(s)/service(s) you will be offering)

9. **Financial Projection** (Provide a breakdown of projected turnover and profit for Year 1 to Year 3)

    Year 1:

    Year 2:

    Year 3:

10. **Contact Us** (Your details e.g. name and email)

There is a downloadable business plan guide in the playbook at:

www.stateofmindplaybook.com.

———

CHAPTER EIGHT

PRINCIPLE #4: CELEBRATE SUCCESS AND LEARN FROM MISTAKES

Acknowledging our success and learning from our mistakes are a necessity for moving forward in business. Both serve us well to move us closer to our goals, so it's worth approaching them both with a positive state of mind. If you find you do not take time to celebrate your wins and you are not positive about your mistakes, then you will be able to change this by the end of the chapter. You will start to see that it's worth celebrating your achievements, whilst lessons will be seen more as opportunities to learn and grow.

What Is Success, and What Does Success Mean to You?

> ## Definition
>
> **Success:** the achieving of the results wanted or hoped for.

Success is very personal, so it's essential to define clearly what it means to you. Firstly, what is success to you? Would you know how to recognise it?

To celebrate success, you need to know and recognise when you achieve success. This comes back to your vision board, goal setting and all the little wins on the way. Success will be different for everyone, and we all have our own journey. The essential point to understand is that we know what success means to us when we achieve it.

Referring to the definition above, success for me is about achievements. Not just one, but all the actions taken that lead to a positive outcome along the way. For example, in figure skating, if I mastered a jump I had been practising for months, then I would celebrate. When a skating performance went well and I achieved a personal best, but I didn't win, I would also celebrate. It was always important to celebrate what went well. In property investing, I celebrate if we get planning permission or an offer accepted. Celebrating also helps you stay motivated to carry on, keeping you in flow because you are enjoying the journey.

A great addition I have made for celebrating success in business is to have a success jar. Each time I have a win or do something successfully, I write it down on a piece of paper, fold it up, and add it to the success jar. Follow the steps in the exercise section of this chapter to create your own success jar.

Why Is the Success Jar Important?

Perhaps you are thinking, why is a success jar so important to my business journey? Will it work? It sounds so simple, really? Well, it reminds you of all the positive and successful things you are doing and achieving that need recognition, but that you may otherwise overlook. Sometimes, it's easy to focus on what we haven't done, I'm sure most people can relate to this. By using the success jar, we can see the progress we have made towards our goals whenever we look at the jar. This gets us feeling positive, motivated and happy.

Sometimes I reward myself for showing up! Perhaps stepping out of my comfort zone, or if a site visit went well, then I will add this to the success jar. What I have found to work really well is to review them all at set intervals. I often do this at the end of the year, or sometimes randomly pick one out to remind myself of successes I have had.

This exercise really helps you understand what success is and what it means to you, and for that reason, it is a powerful exercise.

Core Values

You can measure success by staying true to your core values; that is, what matters to you and your business.

I've shared my values below; however, yours could be different.

My Core Values

Ethics: it really matters that both myself and my company act ethically. Being ethical with property transactions, vendors, tenants, clients, and everyone in my life. This is about having moral principles that governs all my behaviour and all of what I do.

Respect: this is about treating others the way they would like to be treated.

Integrity: to know and do what I believe is the right thing to do.

Sportsmanship: always bringing my best to all competitions.

Family: I value my family and the people I care about.

It's essential to focus on what matters to you and remove things that don't. The reason for doing this is to remove the clutter from your mind so that you are able to free up space for what you value in your life.

Now it's your turn to define your core values. Go to the exercises section in this chapter to complete your core values. Then follow on to the next section below to start learning from your mistakes.

Learn From Mistakes

Although it's important to celebrate the successes and know what success is, it's also equally important to acknowledge mistakes so that you have an opportunity to learn and grow. However, too often, we focus on the mistake rather than learning from these mistakes. The learnings and opportunities they bring can take us closer to our goal. With each iteration, we improve and find out what didn't work, so that we can try new things and achieve our desired outcome. So, how can we use mistakes in the best way possible to help us?

Tip #9: Mistakes are opportunities to learn and grow.

What Is a Mistake?

Definition

Mistake: an action, decision, or judgement that produces an unwanted or unintentional results.

From the definition above, we understand that a mistake is something that gives us an unwanted result. However, the great part about this is that we find ourselves further forward after trying, making a mistake and finding out what didn't work. We can then use this information positively to try new and different ways to help us succeed.

However, before we can learn from the mistakes we make, the first step is to own the mistake, accept responsibility for it and our part in what the end result is. Until you are ready to know that you will make mistakes and be ready to admit that you have made a mistake, you will not be prepared to improve and seek new ways forward. Agree to own your mistakes now and in the future before you proceed with this chapter.

Tip #10: Own your mistakes.

Another important point about making mistakes is that we need to make sure we learn from them, so that we do not risk repeating them in the future. In property investing, these can be costly, so it's important not to make the same expensive mistakes again and again. An excellent way to help you do this is to record and understand these mistakes by creating a lessons learned log. There is a template at the end of this chapter to create your own lessons learned log. I've also included the link to download the playbook online that has a lessons learned log template (www.stateofmindplaybook.com).

A lesson learned log will help you to record lessons as you undertake projects. The idea here is that you will use these lessons to help you refine your processes, record the actions you take to run more smoothly, to be less costly, and more successful in the future due to previous learnings. Understanding your mistakes will mean developing wisdom to make good decisions and choices over time. This will lead to good judgment that will only grow if you genuinely learn from your mistakes.

Here are three examples of lessons learned from my property business journey to help you:

1. Ensure a separate landlord electricity supply: if you are converting an office to flats, for example, or creating a unit in one building, you are likely to have communal areas and need new electricity supplies to those areas for lighting etc. We learnt that we needed to add an additional landlord supply into the building so that our tenant does not pay for our light in the communal hallway. A separate supply ensures you are charged.

2. Organise building warranties upfront: for example, ABC+ or NHBC. You will need to have a structural warranty to get a mortgage, and it's easier to organise this as soon as you can. Otherwise, you may have to rely only on a retrospective architects certificate that is not acceptable to all lenders, thus greatly reducing refinancing or sale options.

3. Only do works to a property that add value or are a tenant requirement: it can be easy to get carried away with what to

refurbish on a project, however, we learnt to always ensure we are either adding value for a sale or adding something that will attract our ideal tenant to make the property easier to rent.

From the examples above, you can understand that the lessons recorded have allowed us to make significant changes to our property business. By recording all of your lessons in your business, you can get the same result, avoiding making the same mistakes repeatedly and improving your business from now on.

Tip #11: Learning from your mistakes are great ways to make your business better.

Closing Quotes

A great quote about success from Ralph Waldo Emerson:
"To laugh often and much; to win the respect of intelligent people and affection of children; to earn the appreciation of honest critics and endure the betrayal of false friends; to appreciate beauty, to find the best in others, to leave the world a little bit better, whether by a healthy child, a garden patch or a redeemed social condition; to know even one life has breathed easier because you have lived. This is to have succeeded."

A powerful quote about mistakes from Paul Bear Bryant:

"When you make a mistake, there are only three things you should ever do about it: admit it, learn from it and don't repeat it."

Exercises: Principle #4

Exercise #1: Success

Define what success means for you:

_____

_____

_____

_____

_____

Exercise #2: The Success Jar

Here are some steps to follow to create your success jar:

1. Buy a clear jar and place it somewhere you will see it every day, either in your office or a place in your home that works well for you.

2. Next, buy some coloured memo paper to write out your successes when you achieve them. Perhaps you could choose different colours to represent different areas of your life or projects you are working on. For example: we have blue for personal achievements and green for property.

3. When you next achieve a success write it down on your memo paper and place it in the jar.

4. Review your success memos as and when you wish, I recommend setting a routine for every 3 months and at the end of the year.

5. I usually replace my jar yearly, but choose a timeframe that works for you. I suggest not more than a couple of years, as your jar will

become cluttered and you need to keep on achieving to keep filling up your jar!

Exercise #3: Core Values

The core value options provided in this exercise have been adapted from the Taproot website (www.taproot.com).

Step One: to find out what your core values are, look at the list below. Read through each of these and choose the core values that connect with you. Try not to overthink them. If you think of a core value that matters to you that is not on the list, then do write that one down too.

The words in bold are the ones I connected with when I completed this exercise as an example.

A

Abundance, Acceptance, Accountability, **Achievement**, Advancement, Adventure, Advocacy, **Ambition**, Appreciation, Attractiveness, Autonomy, Authenticity, Authority

B

Being the Best, Benevolence, Boldness, Brilliance, **Balance, Beauty**

C

Calmness, Caring, Challenge, Charity, Cheerfulness, Cleverness, Community, **Commitment, Compassion**, Cooperation, **Collaboration, Consistency**, Contribution, **Creativity**, Credibility, Curiosity, Citizenship, Competency

D

Daring, Decisiveness, **Dedication**, Dependability, Diversity, **Determination**

E

Encouragement, Enthusiasm, **Ethics**, **Excellence**, Expressiveness, **Empathy**

F

Family, Friendships, Flexibility, **Freedom, Fun, Fairness**, Faith, Fame

G

Generosity, Grace, Growth

H

Happiness, Health, Honesty, Humility, Humour, Harmony

I

Inclusiveness, Independence, Individuality, Innovation, **Inspiration, Intelligence**, Influence, Intuition

J

Joy, Justice

K

Kindness, Knowledge

L

Leadership, Learning, **Love**, Loyalty

M

Making a Difference, Mindfulness, Motivation, Meaningful work

O

Optimism, Open-mindedness, Originality, **Openness**

P

Passion, Performance, Personal Development, Proactive, Professionalism, Peace, Pleasure, Poise, Perfection, Playfulness, Popularity, Power, Preparedness, Proactivity, Punctuality

Q

Quality

R

Recognition, Risk Taking, Recognition, Relationships, **Reliability, Resilience**, Resourcefulness, **Responsibility**, Responsiveness, Religion, Reputation, **Respect**

S

Safety, Security, Service, Spirituality, Stability, Self-respect, Status, Security, Self-control, Selflessness, Simplicity, Stability, **Success, Sportsmanship**

T

Teamwork, **Thankfulness, Thoughtfulness**, Traditionalism, **Trustworthiness**

U

Understanding**, Uniqueness**, Usefulness

V

Versatility, Vision

W

Warmth, Wealth, Well-being, Wisdom

Z

Zeal

Step Two: from the list of values you highlighted above, go through them and pick out the ones that most resonate with you or are most important . Then shortlist them similar to the list below.

For example:

Achievement, Balance, Beauty, Calmness, Caring, Challenge, Charity, Commitment, Compassion, Collaboration, Consistency, Creativity, Dedication, Determination, Ethics, Excellence, Empathy, Family, Freedom, Fun, Fairness, Happiness, Health, Inspiration, Intelligence, Integrity, Kindness, Knowledge, Love, Making a Difference, Mindfulness, Motivation, Openness, Passion, Personal Development, Proactive, Professionalism, Quality, Resilience, Respect, Success, Sportsmanship, Thankfulness, Thoughtfulness, Uniqueness, Warmth, Wealth, Well-being

Step Three: now group the words into those that have similar meaning. I would suggest 5 or 6 groups should be about right. See the list below. Then within each group, choose one word to highlight that you feel represents the best label for the whole group. Once again, do not overthink your labels, as there are no right or wrong answers for this exercise. It's just important that the answer you are defining is the right one for you.

The example below is my groups and I have highlighted my best label for a group:

1. Intelligence, Quality, Excellence, Knowledge, Success, Achievement, Wealth, Personal Development, **Integrity**
2. Happiness, Fun, Well-being, Health, Balance, Beauty, **Making a Difference**, Charity, Freedom, Uniqueness
3. Empathy, **Ethics**, Fairness, Mindfulness
4. **Respect,** Thoughtfulness, Love, Compassion, Openness, Warmth, Thankfulness, Kindness, Caring
5. **Sportsmanship**, Professionalism, Motivation, Proactive, Resilience, Inspiration, Dedication, Determination, Commitment, Collaboration, Consistency, Creativity, Challenge, Calmness, Passion, Integrity
6. **Family**

These will be your Core Values!

Exercise #4: Lessons Learned Log

Note down lessons learned from your business journey so far. Make it a living document. A lessons learned log can be created in Word, Excel or written down. As an example, ideally your lessons learned log should contain the following information:

Lesson Number: _____

Date: _____

Project: _____

Mistake:

_____

_____

_____

_____

_____

Lesson:

_____

_____

_____

_____

_____

Notes for Next Time:

_____

_____

_____

_____

_____

When completing the lessons learned log, it's worth asking the following questions in the notes so that you logically learn a new way forward for next time:

- What was the mistake?
- How did the mistake happen?
- What was my key learning from this mistake?
- What would I improve for next time?

The lessons learned log template is in the playbook and can be downloaded at: www.stateofmindplaybook.com.

CHAPTER NINE

PRINCIPLE #5: PERSISTENCE AND RESILIENCE

When you think of persistence and resilience, what comes to mind? Often, we think of someone who relentlessly picks themselves up and carries on, with the ability to keep going until they succeed. Let's explore these definitions in turn, starting with persistence.

What Is Persistence?

> ### Definition
>
> **Persistence:** continuing a course of action or an opinion despite challenges, issues or opposition.

Persistence is like a secret weapon, an invisible superpower that helps drive someone to get success. People with persistence will keep on moving towards their goals despite any setbacks they may face, as their desire is strong. They have the faith to pursue their goals with a clear plan of action to achieve success.

Persistence in Figure Skating

When thinking about persistence in figure skating, what comes to mind is to continue towards my goal despite any problems I was facing, even if it wasn't easy. This was getting back up off the ice if I had fallen over and to keep on going, even if I didn't want to. Take a competition scenario, for instance, if you gave up after a few jumps went wrong in a programme, you gave up on reaching your goal, which was either to win or get the highest place possible in the competition. I had several competitions when the performance didn't go to plan; I started with a few missed jumps, but then overcame this to execute several good jumps and spins.

Perhaps I didn't win, but I do remember getting a medal on one of these occasions. If I fell on a jump, I was taught to get back up and do the next one. It was a different jump, a new jump that didn't have anything to do with the one before, unless I chose in my mind that it did. My goal was to finish my programme with the best performance, focusing on the task at hand and getting the highest score possible. Moreover, I learnt what went well and what didn't go so well so that I could improve for the next competition.

How Does Persistence Help in Business?

It's widely documented that people often give up in both sport and business just before they are about to be successful or get a break though. Basically, they often give up too soon because they expect sport or entrepreneurship to be easier than they thought, and they are often surprised to find out that, in reality, this is not true. Being an entrepreneur is not easy, or a way to get rich quick, and you need to put in the effort to build a profitable business.

When people realise the effort and commitment required, then enthusiasm can be quickly lost along with faith. They give up too soon! A lack of persistence can be one of the most common reasons for failure in business. With just a little more persistence and a little more effort, you get a little closer to your goal. Those people who persist no matter what obstacle is in their way will eventually succeed. Therefore, it is in your best interest to turn these obstacles into steppingstones to reach your destination.

If success was easy, then everyone would just snap their fingers and be an overnight success with little or no effort. It may seem like an attractive proposition to be an instant or overnight success. However, I believe the Universe has found a way to separate those who are serious about achieving their goals, and people who are just passing the time by making their new business venture a hobby or expecting a get rich quick option. Obstacles may seem like roadblocks, but I think they test how much we really want to achieve something. Those who decide to persist and make progress even when they don't feel like it will be rewarded. When you do finally attain your goal, it gives you great satisfaction and feels amazing. This means that the only way to reach our goals is to put in the required effort, work smart and keep persisting, no matter what obstacles you face, until you achieve what you deserve.

Who Has Shown a Level of Persistence to Achieve Their Goals?

Henry Ford: before finally achieving one of the most successful automotive companies we currently know, he failed and became broke five times.

Elon Musk: before making Space X a success, he attempted three failed rocket launches. This came with great financial loss. Financial documents suggest the likely cost to be hundreds of millions of dollars.

How to Become More Persistent

The first step to becoming persistent is to have a clearly defined TOP goal. The one you set out as per your vision board. At this stage, review your vision board and ensure you have a firm TOP goal. To succeed with your business goals, agree with yourself now that you can only move forward, failures are just opportunities to learn. As per the previous Chapter Eight, Principle #4: Celebrate Success and Learn From Mistakes, let's reiterate this to make sure that you persist with working towards your TOP goal. This principle is very important!

Revisit the exercises you completed in Chapter Five, Principle #1: Desire and Reason Why to ensure you are clear that you have the desire to achieve your TOP goal. This is something you feel deep inside that no one else can know. Do you have that feeling? This desire will keep you going when facing challenges and will stop you from giving up too soon.

Check Chapter Seven, Principle #3: Routine to be sure that you have clear plans and actions so that you never get lost. Use this opportunity to check out how far you have come since you started. Then going forward, make a point to check in regularly with your desire, TOP goal, lessons, and celebrations, and make it part of your routine to do this.

What is Resilience?

Definition
Resilience: the capacity to recover quickly from difficulties; toughness.

Resilience is our capacity to recover swiftly from issues and problems that arise. It is a mental toughness. Our ability to recover quickly from difficulties matters in business and determines how we progress. If we allow ourselves to dwell on issues or not find solutions to problems to overcome them, we can inhibit our growth. On the other hand, resilient people in business are able to learn from mistakes, recover quickly, and move on. However, this mental toughness seems to be easier for some, and those people seem to be able to cope better with life's challenges than others. This therefore raises the question of whether resilience is nature or nurture. In other words, is resilience something we are born with, or can we learn it to be more resilient in our life?

Can We Learn Resilience?

As a figure skater, sometimes these questions were raised:

- Is resilience something that one is born with, or was it something that could be learned or developed over time?

- Is mental toughness something one can develop, or are people born with it?

As I mentioned earlier, all the principles in this book can be learned, but this one can be more difficult for some people and easier for others. However, the good news is that extensive research evidence has shown that the skill of resilience can be learned by everyone even if it is not easy. When we experience emotional pain, suffer a loss or have a major trauma in our lives, we can develop resilience. Therefore, it is possible to develop a resilient state of mind. This is something I learned and developed from childhood growing up as a figure skater.

How I Learned Resilience

I learned resilience at a young age due to being in a competitive sport. If a jump didn't work, I would fall over and would need to get back up from the ice, tweak an arm or leg position, and try again. I was constantly refining until I could execute the jump correctly. Each time I got up from the ice to try again, I was learning resilience without realising; I understood that each iteration got me closer to my goal. Sometimes this process would take hours and hours of practise over several months. This was an excellent lesson for my property investing business, that focused practice with persistence and resilience over time, gets results.

> # Tip #12: Focused practice with persistence and resilience over time gets results.

Resilience in Business

When starting your own business, it can seem like an exciting journey but also a long one. It takes time to build a business, with challenges to overcome, and a considerable amount of resilience is necessary to keep going. I have met many challenges, planning hurdles, builder issues, and it can be easy to give up. I have also seen other investors overwhelmed, or who have faced challenges and have given up too early. Working to overcome issues and problem solving constantly is so essential as an entrepreneur. Therefore, practising resilience is important as it can really help you to keep working on your business goals and not give up. This means we need to understand how we can be more resilient.

How to Be More Resilient

To do this, we can model the resilient behaviour of successful people. When we look back, we can see that many great inventions were created due to resilient thinking. Further, many great athletes who achieved Olympic gold medals also adopted resilient behaviour. Let's look at some examples:

Thomas Edison: an inventor in the 20th century. He spent most of his time understanding what didn't work. He spent most of his life failing, there were tens and thousands of failures, in fact. However, Thomas Edison never gave up. He learnt from all tens of thousands of his mistakes, and this led to the light bulb, among other things. This is a lesson to us all to never give up, as each time we learn what didn't work, we get a step closer to what will work.

Torvill and Dean: these Olympic UK figure skaters are a superb example of resilience. I have been fortunate to watch them practise with my own eyes. They would tirelessly practise the same move for hours and hours, however long it took, never giving up. It was magical to watch as they figured out each step, worked together as a team and kept going until they perfected whatever move they were doing. With each step, they got better, and there is no doubt that once they had mastered a move, it was true perfection.

So, if we know what makes these people resilient, then it is possible that we too can start to practise their behaviour by adding this into our routines and habits to be more resilient ourselves. Let's look closer at what makes a person resilient so that we can model this behaviour.

Psychologists and experts, including resilience specialist Glenn Schiraldi (2017), have studied successful people such as athletes, inventors and business leaders to find that they all have resilient traits and characteristics. These successful people have learned and developed to build a resilient state of mind. Resilience is learned and coached not only in elite sport, but in all sport, I can certainly vouch for that. I can recall learning to be resilient and also helping young athletes develop resilient qualities. Steven M Southwick and Dennis Charney in their book Resilience - The Science of Mastering Life's Greatest Challenges, found resilient traits by studying people who were prisoners of war and in Army Special Forces. They managed to thrive in these extremely stressful situations and were resilient over and over again. All the above present examples of where people have had to be resilient to survive, thrive and succeed, so the question we need the answer to now is, what are these traits? I have summarised the most common ten traits or characteristics that I feel that have helped me the most from sport to business below.

Ten Common Traits of a Resilient State of Mind

1. Optimism and positivity, the confidence about your success in the future.

2. Seeing failure as feedback and learning opportunities, celebrating achievements.

3. The ability to control emotions and be calm under pressure.

4. Being flexible in their approach, adapting and pivoting in new situations.

5. Focusing on what they can control and acting based on this.

6. Thinking about what works well and focusing attention on doing more of these actions.

7. Planning and executing effective solutions.

8. Focusing on a goal, vision and purpose.

9. Forging positive and supportive relationships with like-minded people.

10. The ability to focus their attention.

Some of these traits you may recognise in the state of mind principles, meaning that working on the other principles in this book also means you will become more resilient. This is about developing your thoughts, beliefs, behaviours and attitudes to build a resilient state of mind to apply to your business.

As mentioned above, if we know what these traits are, we can learn to model them. Here are some examples of how these can be applied to your business:

- What have you have achieved in your business in the last week?

For example, an offer accepted or planning permission granted. It doesn't matter how long it took; focus on the outcome. This also forms part of your routine by reflecting on what you achieved.

- What is going well in your business?
  Look at what is going well so that you can model your behaviour to do more of the same. For example, if a strategy works well for you, you will notice specific actions that get you a positive result. It's worth noting these actions down, for example, in a spreadsheet so you can do more of this.

- What is in your control?
  It's always important to work where we have control, as sometimes things happen on projects that are out of our control. However, we can control how we act in all situations and, for example, we can choose who to have as part of our power team.

Resilience in business can also be developed further when you have supportive relationships and a positive network of family, friends and fellow entrepreneurs around you. When you have strong connections in your personal and business life, you are more resistant to overwhelm and stress as you gain a sense of belonging and self-worth. Therefore, it's a great idea to surround yourself with like-minded people who are supportive and positive, who you can problem-solve with to help you on your journey.

Tip #13: Surround yourself with positive and supportive people.

Whatever we wish to call them, perhaps mistakes, failures, or challenges, they can either be seen as hindering our progress or as ways to learn what doesn't work to progress. Let's look at how we can explain setbacks to ourselves and start to view them more positively.

How Do We Explain Setbacks to Ourselves? The 3Ps!

If I failed a test in figure skating, the focus would be on understanding what errors I made that I could learn from and not repeat next time. The feedback was constructive and conducted in a way to help me pass the test next time. This was seen as a temporary setback and that I could improve to pass the test next time. This wouldn't mean that I wasn't any good at figure skating, just that I needed to learn to be better to get to the next level and compete with those at the next level.

A leading psychologist, Martin Seligman, says the way that we explain setbacks to ourselves is really important. He states that dealing with challenges can be made up of three main elements of optimism, also known as the 3Ps:

1. Permanence – Seeing bad events as temporary rather than permanent. So, rather than saying, "My business partner never likes anything I do", you could reframe this as, "My business partner didn't like my ideas this time."

2. Pervasiveness – Not to let setbacks in one area of your life affect other completely unrelated areas of your life. So, rather than saying, "I'm not good at using spreadsheets", you can reframe this as, "There is more to life than spreadsheets."

3. Personalisation – Do not blame yourself when a bad situation occurs. View the circumstances or other outside factors that may be the possible cause, rather than making it personal. So, rather

than saying, "I didn't get an offer accepted because I'm hopeless at negotiation", you can reframe this to, "My offer didn't get accepted because someone offered higher than my business case would allow."

It's possible to use the 3Ps above to look at the way 'good' or 'bad' situations are described under an optimistic and pessimistic viewpoint, as shown in the table below (Peterson, 2006):

Optimist

Good Situation	Bad Situation
Permanent	Temporary
Pervasive	Specific
Personal	External Causes

Pessimist

Good Situation	Bad Situation
Temporary	Permanent
Specific	Pervasive
External Causes	Personal

As you can see above, the optimist believes the good situation to be permanent and the bad situation temporary. I love reframing situations using the 3Ps and I believe that if you haven't tried this already then try it now. Use the 3Ps when thinking about a bad situation you have experienced recently in your business or life, then reframe it. When you complete Exercise #6, at the end of this chapter, you will see here that I have refined and adapted this further to help deal with difficult situations in your business journey. You can use this exercise as many times as you wish and whenever you need to reframe difficult situations.

What If You Think You Are Not Very Resilient?

Sometimes when we think of the word resilience, we may think of challenges and setbacks in our life that have been difficult to recover from. If you are thinking about these types of situations, then you are most likely to be resilient, as you have 'bounced back' from a difficult situation. Resilience is not about people who are unaffected by the challenges that life brings, this is not resilience. Being resilient is our ability to get back up and carry on again and again when faced with setbacks.

Resilience is the ability to adapt, and I believe that we can all adapt to demonstrate resilience. We know that some people may be more resilient than others, but it is not an unchangeable quality that you either have or don't have. Resilience is a learned ability and one that you can build to get the results you want and to get success in your business.

> Tip #14: Resilience is not the absence of challenge or difficulty. Resilience is the ability to adapt and grow following adversity.

Resilience in Sport Applied to Business

As mentioned earlier in this chapter, resilience has been a key principle applied from figure skating directly to my property investing business. In sport, coaches work diligently with athletes to learn, develop and apply resilience to overcome the many challenges in sport so they can be successful. Therefore, it is worth considering how this coaching helps deliver the amazing results that we see in sport and how we can apply the same state of mind methods to succeed in business. One thing that is certain, sportspeople do not settle for an average state of mind. Therefore, to get the same result and level of success as professional sportspeople, we should apply a resilient state of mind to our business. Being resilient matters, because learning to be resilient in your business is learning how to be a successful entrepreneur. If we give up on the quest to learn resilience, we accept defeat. Try using the exercises at the end of this chapter to develop your resilience, so that you can apply this to your business journey, get amazing results and become the champion of your business!

Resilient Thoughts

Resilience is about recovering quickly from setbacks, and being successful means learning and developing your resilient behaviours to apply to your business. You definitely need to be resilient as an entrepreneur to keep going, problem solve, and understand that you get closer to the end result with each iteration, no matter how many times you try.

You can apply the ten qualities and the 3Ps of improving resilience to the exercises shared at the end of this chapter. These are the exercises I have found to be the most helpful from 30 years of sport and 15 years of professional sports coaching that I have applied to property investing. I have chosen these exercises as I believe they will develop your resilience, help you overcome challenges and get the best results possible. Don't forget to read the quote below and then go to the exercises section of this chapter so that you can start building your resilience.

Closing Quotes

"If I had to select one quality, one personal characteristic that I regard as being most highly correlated with success, whatever the field, I would pick the trait of persistence. The will to endure to the end, to get knocked down seventy times and get up off the floor saying, 'Here comes number seventy-one!'"

Richard M. Devos

"Resilience is knowing that you are the only one that has the power and the responsibility to pick yourself up."

Mary Holloway

Exercises: Principle #5

Developing resilience is a personal journey, so it's important to determine what will work for you to define your own resilience strategy.

Resilience exercises are ways we can develop our resilience and build mental toughness. By answering the questions that follow, resilience skills can be learned through small, incremental wins, and you can develop routines and habits that will form the foundation of your resilient state of mind. When the going gets tough in your business, this level of resilience will really matter to keep you going. Remember, though, that focused practice is important to enhancing resilience.

Exercise #1 — Previous Experience

How do you boost resilience and meet challenges that you may face with confidence and the ability to succeed, even after a failure? This exercise helps you to look back and focus on your past experiences with a resilient state of mind.

Think about a time in your life that has been challenging. How did you respond in this situation?

Once you have this, then answer these questions:

1. What result did you achieve?

_____

_____

_____

_____

_____

2. What was your goal?

_____

_____

_____

_____

_____

3. What were the challenges you faced?

_____

_____

_____

_____

_____

4. Can you recall any negative thoughts that you had?

_____

_____

_____

_____

_____

5. Did anyone help you?

_____

_____

_____

_____

6. What was your attitude to overcome your challenges?

_____

_____

_____

_____

7. What were your strengths?

_____

_____

_____

_____

8. What skills did you use that helped you the most?

_____

_____

_____

_____

From 1-10, how would you rate your resilience to this challenge? (circle or highlight)

1   2   3   4   5   6   7   8   9   10

If you did not rate yourself as 10, what could you improve next time to overcome a similar challenge?

_____

_____

_____

_____

_____

Think of a business challenge.

Look at your answer for each question above to help you understand what resilience skills you already have and how you can improve on those in the future to meet this business challenge. This exercise will hopefully show you that you have been resilient in the past, and therefore you will be able to be resilient with the challenges that running a business will bring you in the future, and you will be able to overcome these challenges with resilience.

Exercise #2 – Evaluate Your Resilience: How Resilient Are You?

Now you have established your previous resilience, the next step is to understand how resilient you are right now. In order to be more resilient, you need to have a starting point, a baseline, so that you can measure your improvement. This exercise will also help you understand what skills you have and those that need work. To increase your resilience, you need to know what areas of resilience you will focus on.

From 1-10, rate yourself on the following questions (1 being the worst and 10 being the best):

1. How do you accept yourself for who you are?

1   2   3   4   5   6   7   8   9   10

2. How good are you at coping with challenges?

1   2   3   4   5   6   7   8   9   10

3. How good are you at problem solving?

1   2   3   4   5   6   7   8   9   10

4. How confident are you when dealing with challenging situations?

1   2   3   4   5   6   7   8   9   10

5. How are your communication skills when working with others in challenging times?

1   2   3   4   5   6   7   8   9   10

Review your scores.

Add up your total score and write it below.

TOTAL SCORE: _____

Look at your ratings for each question. Did you rate any questions as 1?

If you did, think about what you could do to move this rating to a 2 or 3. What steps could you take?

_____

_____

_____

_____

_____

If any questions scored between 2-4, think about what steps you could take to move you closer to 5.

_____

_____

_____

_____

_____

Do you have any at 5 or higher? Great! Think about how you could raise these to 6, 7 or even a 10. What steps would you take?

_____

_____

_____

_____

_____

This exercise will help you understand how resilient you are right now and what steps you can take to improve.

Exercise #3 — Gratitude

I keep a gratitude journal that I recite every day. I have ten things I am grateful for, and then I add one for that particular day. It's really easy to do and a proven method to increase your resilience. To start practising gratitude, write down something every day that you are grateful for. Try it below.

I am grateful for:

1. _____

_____

2. _____

_____

3. _____

_____

4. _____

_____

5. _____

_____

Exercise #4 — Ending the Day Well

End your day by reflecting on and writing down what you achieved. Note how you felt, did you lose track of time, was it challenging or effortless, did you feel in control?

_____

_____

_____

_____

_____

Exercise #5 — Mental Toughness

Jason Selk is a performance coach who has trained a range of Olympic and professional athletes. He used the following exercise to increase mental toughness that will only take a few minutes of your day:

First, try this centring breathing cycle:
1. Start with a centring breath.
2. Breathe in slowly.
3. Hold it for a few seconds.
4. Breathe out slowly.

Next, write a personal identity statement that either emphasises a positive quality that you have or specifies something you want to achieve, such as 'I am a successful property investor.'

Personal Identity Statement:

_____

_____

_____

_____

_____

Then, visualise your personal highlight reel:

1. Think of three things you have achieved yesterday.

    1.

    2.

    3.

2. Mentally visualise three important things you need to do today.

    1.

    2.

    3.

3. Repeat your identity statement for five seconds.

4. Finish with another centring breath cycle as above.

Exercise #6— 3Ps for Changing Your Perspective

1. Pick a challenging business experience that is happening right now.

2. Go to the template in the next section.

3. Use the template to note down how you think about this experience as per the 3Ps.

Then, reframe it using the next section of the template.

For example:

Issue: you renovated a house and you haven't sold it in 3 months.

Section 1

Personal: I am not good enough and I didn't do a good enough renovation.

Permanent: I will never sell the house.

Pervasive: I also failed my family as a husband, wife or parent.

Section 2

External: the property market has dipped recently. The property didn't meet with buyers' needs.

Temporary: I will sell the house and there are some actions I can take to help me do that.

Specific: this applies only to property investing and has nothing to do with family life.

Template:

Issue: _____

_____

Section 1

Personal: _____

_____

Permanent: _____

_____

Pervasive: _____

_____

Section 2

External: _____

_____

Temporary: _____

_____

Specific: _____

_____

CHAPTER TEN

PRINCIPLE #6: POSITIVE ATTITUDE... WITH AN ELEMENT OF REALISM

This principle is about accepting that our business will not always go to plan, things won't always go our way, but it's how we deal with these challenges that help us move forward in our business in a positive way.

What is a Positive Attitude?

A positive attitude is a way of thinking and a state of mind that has a vision of a favourable outcome. It is the mental attitude of visualising success and good results, and the openness and willingness to try new things. This means focusing on the positive aspects of our life rather than the negatives. It's a state of mind that brings light and happiness to those who possess it.

Here's a great definition from Kendra Cherry at Very Well Mind (2017):

"Approaching life's challenges with a positive outlook. It does not necessarily mean avoiding or ignoring the bad things; instead, it involves making the most of the potentially bad situations, trying to see the best in other people, and viewing yourself and your abilities in a positive light."

Although this principle focuses on how we can positively progress in our business, it is not about how you can be positive all the time, as this is not the life of an entrepreneur and not realistic. How we deal with both positive and negative situations in our business really matters and impacts on how we can move forward with a positive state of mind.

What is Realism?

> ## Definition
>
> **Realism:** the attitude or practise of accepting a situation as it is and being prepared to deal with it accordingly.

This is understanding that not everything goes our way, and that's ok; it's how we deal with this practically and sensibly. Being realistic about who we are, how we are, our emotions and how we can deal with these emotions help us develop a positive attitude. We must let ourselves deal with frustrations first so that we give ourselves time to deal with emotions, meaning that we can move forward in our business in a positive way.

Tip #15: Deal with your emotions first before you start to problem solve.

How Do We Deal With Life's Challenges So That We Can Move Forward in a Positive Way?

When I was a figure skater, I would practise a move over and over again. If I was learning a jump, for example, practising by myself, I might start patiently remembering to learn from each jump that wasn't quite working. This method would be great if I tweaked each repetition, and then I landed the jump. I had finally mastered what I needed to do to execute this jump correctly. However, what happened when I kept trying and failing? Perhaps I had tried fifty times or more and nothing seemed to work? Apart from being bruised physically and having a sore butt, I would keep trying. As I got more and more frustrated, my ability to be positive and to make a useful contribution to each iteration would be clouded by anger, frustration and negativity. Essentially by emotion. Have you ever experienced this with a task or a situation? Think back to a time where you may have experienced something similar? Got it? Read on...

So, what happens if you carry on in this frustrated, angry manner? Does the task get easier? Do you start to improve, or do you think this is a waste of time and energy as this is not purposeful practice?

When my coach would see that a particular move was degrading because my practice was not positive or adding value to correcting a mistake and making an element work, he would call me for a 'time out'. This 'time out' would be 10 minutes to leave the ice and do something else. The time could be to have a drink, go for a walk, take my skates off and relax; it was my choice in how I spent that time, but it could not be on the ice. I would usually have a mini-rant to myself to lose the frustration, then relax and reflect. The point was that it was time away from the task, to refocus and to deal with emotion so that it was possible to move forward in a more positive way. When returning to the ice, I would be refreshed, ready to try again and have a more positive state of mind in which to do so. A new perspective to try new techniques and take on new information to apply to the movement, jump or spin I was working on.

In my skating life, this would work nearly every time, and I have readily applied this to my working life, personal life, business life and, of course, property life. If a situation or task is becoming difficult, frustrating or is making you angry, it's time to leave the task or situation for now and have a 'time out'. Essentially, taking time to manage your emotions.

You can choose what you do, but examples could be to go for a walk or make a coffee, whatever you would prefer. The important factor here is to take time out and do something in that time that works for you. If you can move forward positively after, you know whatever you did worked well, and you can learn and apply the same principle next time. In my experience, I was given 10 minutes. I believe a time limit can be a good idea as it gives a set time for you to tackle those emotions, and at the end of that time, you need to be ready to move on. If we don't set a time, it can be easy to dwell on our emotions rather than move forward. However, more challenging situations need more time. I've experienced this myself. Be realistic, if you have an issue that you need to sleep on, for example a challenging email, then writing an emotional response as a draft and then tweaking the next day to be more rational may work well in that situation.

Think back to your frustrating situation from earlier; imagine taking time out from that situation. How does that make you feel?

Remember that we are all different, so ensure that you find a way to deal with your emotions that works best for you. After many 'time outs' during my skating life, I found out that what worked for me was sometimes different depending on the situation, but in time I knew what to do and then I would do that same thing each time based on the situation or task. This almost reflects what we covered in Chapter Seven, Principle #3: Routine; the 'time out' should form part of your routine.

How to Apply the 'Time Out' to Your Business

There are many challenges that occur in business and during projects. Sometimes things don't go to plan, take longer and cost more, but that doesn't mean these projects won't be a success. Quite the opposite, in fact, some very challenging projects in property have often been the ones with the most financial reward, given the most lessons and therefore the most opportunities.

To get the project complete in the most efficient way, whilst getting the result that you desire requires managing emotions to move forward in a positive way. Reacting to a problem doesn't solve it. Instead, when something goes wrong, take the 'time out' whenever you need it. If it's time to think or time to release frustration, one thing is certain: you will have more clarity to move forward into problem solving. You will get there quicker with less anguish and a more positive attitude from your power team too. In my experience of working with builders, we get more ideas flowing when I'm not frustrated with some aspects that didn't go to plan. Moreover, they are not frustrated with me! By approaching the problem in the right way with a positive attitude, it's possible to brainstorm ideas and overcome problems more readily.

How to Move Forward

Once you have taken the time to overcome your emotions, you'll be ready to respond to the given situation. Here are three good questions that you can ask yourself and your team when problem solving positively:

1. What might be a better way to do x?
2. What if we/I…?
3. How might we/I…?

Tip #16: Remember that you are in control of how you think, feel and behave.

Situations and problems occur, yes, and not everything goes our way. Our attitude and response to these situations make them either positive or negative. We can choose how we respond, and sometimes how we respond can be determined by our emotions rather than logic. However, we have the power to be in control of how we think and feel, how we deal with our emotions, and we can take control of our situations. It is important to realise, though, that no one else can control this except you, and only you know the right choice to make. So, take the time to think about that choice, take time to get control of your emotions and then the situation. By having control of your emotions, your attitude and your state of mind, you'll then take control of the situation and achieve a successful outcome. Taking control means taking time to allow yourself to have emotions and express them so that you can move on positively with all concerned.

The Power of the 'Time Out'

What is powerful about the 'time out'? It is a simple concept that is very powerful and effective as it allows you to deal with your emotions. This concept is not about ignoring your emotions or brushing them aside. Ignoring our emotions does not make them go away and is not helpful. This is about taking time to focus your attention on dealing with emotions fully, so you are ready to move on. Making mistakes, learning from our mistakes, allowing yourself time to be frustrated by them and then moving on with a fresh new problem-solving approach.

What to Do When Negative Thoughts Dominate Your Mind?

If you become dominated by negative thoughts, frustrated or annoyed, then you cannot focus your mind on 'how do I fix this' or 'what can I do about x?'. You are not thinking about learning, problem solving, solutions or what progress you can make. If you don't deal with this negativity, then your thinking will be affected, and perhaps you'll make some bad choices. This is the perfect time to have a 'time out'.

The exercises in this chapter are really helpful to overcome challenges by taking a 'time out' to control your emotions next time you are feeling frustrated with a situation. This exercise works well for frustrations and problem solving every day, but we may need more time to overcome our emotions and start problem solving for bigger challenges. In this instance, 10-15 minutes may not be enough. Do set more time aside if you need it;

however, I do recommend a time limit as mentioned previously to give you the time needed to be upset, frustrated or angry, so that you have an end time when you will need to move forward. This helps us focus solely on the problem, acknowledge it, and deal with our emotions, but we don't allow ourselves to dwell on our situation.

Closing Quotes

"You are the conductor of your own attitude! Nobody else can compose your thoughts for you."

Lee J. Colan

Exercises: Principle #6

Next time you are having negative thoughts over a problem or setback, perhaps you feel angry or frustrated, try one of the following 10-minute 'time outs':

Exercise #1 — Time Out One

1. Stop what you are doing. Go to a different location with a notepad or phone. For example, if you are in a building, go to the car or a nearby park.

2. Write down ALL the negative thoughts—don't hold back. If it takes less than 10 minutes, then that's ok, end the time out when you are finished, however, no longer than the time set. I would say 15 minutes would be the maximum if you wanted to adjust the time slightly to fit your requirement, but any longer will have you dwelling on the problem and not moving forward.

Negative Thoughts:

_____

_____

_____

_____

_____

3. After 10 minutes look through your list of negative thoughts and ask yourself: are they REALLY ALL true? (Circle/Highlight)

YES/NO

4. Ask yourself the three questions: what might be a better way? What if we/I...? How might we/I...?

    _____

    _____

    _____

    _____

    _____

5. Write down your solutions, options, how to progress, ideas, etc.

    _____

    _____

    _____

    _____

    _____

6. If you have a team, then speak to the team regarding problem solving.

Exercise #2 – Time Out Two

1. Once again, stop what you are doing and go to a different location.

2. Take time to think about all the negative thoughts, what went wrong, allow yourself to be frustrated and have a little rant if you need to. Take 10 minutes once again or less if you finish before then.

3. After 10 minutes, ask yourself: are they REALLY ALL true?

4. Ask yourself the three questions: what might be a better way? What if we/I...? How might we/I...?

5. Think through your ideas, solutions, how to move forward, etc.

6. If you have a team, then speak to the team regarding problem solving.

Try these 'time out' options next time you start having negative thoughts and emotions that are getting in the way of your progress. Over time I'm sure you will see that your positive attitude will start to improve by taking control of your emotions and any negative thoughts. This is a positive attitude with an element of realism approach!

Remember, for bigger challenges increase the time, but do make sure you give yourself a fixed deadline to move on. Be realistic with yourself, the problem you are facing and deal positively with your challenges.

CHAPTER ELEVEN

PRINCIPLE #7: SELF-CONFIDENCE AND SELF-WORTH

Confidence! I've broken down this chapter into two sections. Firstly, 'self', all about self-confidence and self-worth. How this affects your business growth. Secondly, your confidence around money and your financial success in business.

Self-confidence and self-worth are centred around what you believe about yourself and how you value yourself. This is paramount to the success that you want to achieve in your business, as your inner self helps you get the results that you desire in the outside world. That is your vision and your TOP goal. Only you can make this happen, so you need to believe in yourself and value yourself to get results in your business. I will help you do that in this chapter.

We will also explore your confidence in money, your money state of mind and how this can affect being confident with managing your money. The key to investing, securing investment for your business and achieving your financial success is about how confident you are and how you feel about money. So, I will also help you to grow your money state of mind.

Self-Confidence

Let's start with self-confidence and take the time to really understand what the term self-confidence actually means.

Definition

Self-confidence: a feeling of trust in one's abilities, qualities, and judgement.

So, self-confidence is about the belief and faith we have in our own abilities, meaning that self-confidence can, in fact, be self-belief. This is believing that you have the ability to overcome any challenges to succeed. Understanding that you believe and trust your abilities, regardless of any weaknesses you may have or what others may think about you. Do you believe in yourself and have faith in your abilities? Once again, this is a quality that we can learn, develop, and improve over time, so if you think you do not have enough self-confidence, this chapter will help boost your belief in your abilities.

Self-confidence helps you deal with pressure and work through challenges as they arise. Moreover, it is also an attractive quality that will draw other people to you and put them at ease. When people project confidence, it helps them make a great first impression with others and gain credibility. Self-confidence improves all areas of your life and helps you to be more successful. So, if we know that self-confidence helps us to be successful, why don't we practise it more and believe in ourselves more?

One of the reasons can be due to fear, that is, the fear of the unknown or the fear of failure. However, if we take some steps to put ourselves in a situation that we are afraid of, this can help us overcome that fear and assure us that nothing bad will happen. Going forward, we then become more accustomed to the situation. Go to Exercise #1 at the end of this chapter and follow the steps to help you to do something that you are afraid of; this means getting out of your comfort zone to overcome that fear.

> # Tip #17: Put yourself in a situation you are afraid of to help you overcome the fear.

We can also gain self-confidence by achieving, and likewise lose it if we are not achieving. This demonstrates why it is a great idea to set SMART goals and, more importantly, ways to achieve them. By achieving goals and taking steps towards them, we believe ourselves to be competent, which, in turn, increases our self-confidence. Let's understand more about what behaviours we can have, either with high or low self-confidence.

High and Low Self-Confidence

How we behave in situations will differ if we have high or low self-confidence. By looking at a few of the behaviours below, can you identify whether you think you have high or low self-confidence?

1. **High self-confidence** – Being your authentic self (who you really are) and doing what you believe is the right thing, despite what others may think or say about you.

   Low self-confidence – Adjusting your behaviour to please others and based on what you believe others may think of you or say about you.

2. **High self-confidence** – Owning your mistakes and learning from them.

   Low self-confidence – Hiding your mistakes or blaming others when things go wrong.

3. **High self-confidence** – Taking informed risks, being prepared to go outside your comfort zone to achieve more. Not being afraid to fail so that you can learn to succeed.

   Low self-confidence – Not taking any risks, staying within your comfort zone and fearing failure.

The behaviours above are an example to highlight just how important high self-confidence can be when you are faced with tricky situations or challenges, and how your behaviour can have a negative impact if you have low self-confidence. As you can see, people with high self-confidence have a more positive behaviour; they value themselves, readily admit when they are wrong and learn from mistakes.

So, how can you improve your self-confidence so that you exhibit more positive behaviours? From my research, I believe there are five main areas that we can work on to increase our self-confidence to get success:

1. Know and work with your strengths and weaknesses.
2. Focus on your achievements.
3. Have confidence-boosting SMART goals.

4. Know your personal brand and values.

5. Accept that what other people think of you is none of your business.

Let's explore each of these in turn.

1. **Know and work with your strengths and weaknesses**

   Even if you are the most confident person, you can doubt yourself sometimes. As a figure skater, even if I had performed a move several times and knew very well that I could perform it with ease, there were times when I would doubt myself. There were also moves that I would find easier to execute than others, and this would vary from skater to skater. What this taught me is that we all have different strengths and weaknesses that we can use to our advantage. For example, you may be great with ideas but struggle to find solutions to problems. This can cause dips in confidence, and at these times, it is worth finding out what the cause of the problem is.

   A personal SWOT can help you identify the tasks or skills you are good at and show you what your weaknesses are so that you can improve. You can also outsource the tasks that you are not good at so that you can concentrate your attention on where you can add the most value to your business. However, unless you know your weaknesses, you are not able to identify what you are doing well and what areas need work. At this point, go to the exercises section and complete your personal SWOT analysis in Exercise #2. If you are struggling to maintain self-confidence due to things that you cannot do, this exercise will help you to improve.

2. **Focus on your achievements**

   Show yourself evidence of what you have achieved. Go to the exercise section now to complete your achievement list (Exercise #4). Write out your top ten achievements to date in the relevant sections.

   Take time to review these achievements and the tasks that you are good at. Remember to look back at these in times when you start to question your abilities with any negative self-talk that will impact your self-confidence.

3. **Have SMART goals that boost your confidence**

   As we discussed in Chapter Six about goal-oriented individuals and TOP goals, setting and achieving goals helps develop and boost self-confidence.

   It can be helpful to inform your goal setting with your personal SWOT analysis to enhance your self-confidence. You will then know what you are trying to achieve, that your goals and tasks align with your personal strengths, so you can play down any weaknesses, maximise your opportunities and put plans in place to mitigate any threats. This will show you how capable and responsible you are and help you believe that you not only have a plan to achieve your goals, but they are aligned to you as an individual. You will also reassure yourself that you have measures in place to deal with any weaknesses or threats.

4. **Know your personal brand and values**

   When you know your personal brand, you can easily project a positive image of your authentic self to others. By doing this, you will likely receive positive feedback that will further increase your self-confidence.

People with self-confidence live according to their values and ensure they make decisions based on these values. It can be difficult at times, but when looking at the bigger picture, people who believe in themselves will act based on their personal brand and their values, even if they are not easy. All your actions define your character, so before taking any action, it's worth asking what the best version of yourself would do in this situation. What action would they take? What decision would they make? Be sure to look at your values from Chapter Eight and go to the exercises section at the end of this chapter to start building your personal brand.

If you are taking an action that is difficult and perhaps means a short-term sacrifice, but in the long term will align with the best version of yourself, then remember that you will like yourself more and be proud of who you are by being true to your authentic self, your values, who you want to be and your personal brand. Further, taking action that only aligns with your personal brand and values can really help ensure you stay on the right journey to achieve your version of success.

5. **Accept that what others think of you is none of your business**
   Although we may want to appear confident to others, that doesn't mean that everyone will like you or agree with you. There may be some people around you, such as family and friends, who tell you that you can't reach your goal, that your goal is too big, or you are not ready. Although most people are trying to help in these situations, unless they are informed, try not to listen. Often people are wrong and make statements without fully understanding all the

facts. There are people that make a difference in the world every day, and in most cases, these people would also have had others telling them it was not possible. If you think you can do it, you can, so believe in yourself and keep on going.

Also, if you want to please everyone, it is worth taking the time now to note that this is impossible for anyone to do. You will not be aligned with everyone, as we are all different and share different values. Please accept that this is ok, and you will do a great job attracting the people that are 'right' for you.

Tip #18: What others think of you is none of your business.

How Do You Appear More Confident to Other People?

If you are presenting to an audience or potential investors and your head is down, you are constantly fidgeting, appear nervous and keep apologising, your audience will naturally have less confidence in you. Compare this to someone who holds their head high, speaks very clearly and is open and honest when they do not know something. Being confident does inspire confidence in others, and gaining that confidence is key to success.

Self-confident people are often naturally very at ease with themselves and what they do, while also gaining trust and inspiring confidence in others. This usually takes some time and practice to appear outwardly confident, but we can all achieve it. Let's look at how you can use your self-belief and project this on to others so that you can be more effective through body language and creating a great first impression.

Body Language

Your self-confidence is in your body language. The upside of projecting a positive self-image to others is that it will also improve your self-confidence. So, if you appear to have more confidence in yourself, other people will respond better to you, and then this positive feedback from others will help reinforce your confidence further so that you believe in yourself more. This is creating a positive self-confidence cycle rather than a negative one.

To improve your body language, you can:

1. Sit or stand up with good posture in an upright position
2. Adopt an open posture
3. Keep your head up
4. Use open gestures when talking or presenting
5. Keep your palms facing slightly towards your audience

The above sounds simple to do, but do you do it?

Creating a Great First Impression

You can never go back again to meet someone for the first time, so it's important to get it right. Creating a great first impression can be tricky. Meeting someone for the first time or giving a presentation can make you nervous, which can lead you to be unsure or even shy, but it is possible to take some immediate steps so that you appear more confident, such as:

1. Maintain eye contact (do be mindful of cultural differences)

2. Do not fidget; this can make you look nervous
3. Shake hands in a natural way, not too firm and not too weak.

You can take all of the above on board to make some immediate differences to your behaviour when interacting with others. However, the longer-term steps to practise inner self-confidence in the way you behave and interact with others increases how much you trust in your abilities. This will, in turn, reflect on how others perceive you too. By learning and developing this over time, you will increase your self-confidence and the confidence that others have in you as a person. So it's really important to work on what you believe internally and what you project externally with your body language and communication.

Self-Confidence for Outward Projection

People need to have confidence in you and your abilities in order to trust and respect you. You will show this in your behaviour, how you speak, your body language, what you say and how you say it. By projecting confidence, other people are more likely to respond positively.

The key with outward projection is to also have inner belief, so that you do not come across as fake. To be authentic, the confidence you project needs to come from within, and from your brand, values, and achievements. Basically, all of the five areas you have worked on so far in this chapter.

> # Tip #19: The key to outward projection is to have belief so that you are not 'fake'.

Why Is Self-Confidence and Belief Important for Entrepreneurship?

The reason I've included self-confidence is two-fold; it's to help you have the belief state of mind to succeed in your business, and for you to appear confident when interacting with people or presenting to others, like working with investors or vendors, for example. Running a business is often very people-focused, therefore people must trust and have confidence in you.

To be a successful business owner, you need to have confidence in yourself to achieve. This is about having confidence and belief in your ability to run a successful business by utilising all the knowledge you have learnt to take action and overcome any fears. By working on your self-confidence in this chapter, you will start to become more confident in yourself and your abilities to get started, get out of your comfort zone and take the steps required to grow your business.

How a Belief State of Mind Can Help Your Business Succeed

Self-confidence and belief can also help others have confidence in you. This will help you potentially secure investment finance as well as helping you build rapport with customers, vendors, and your 'power team'.

Whilst it is very important to know your business and your numbers back to front and inside out, you also need to believe in yourself and your business when presenting to a potential investor. They will be investing in your business and trusting in you, so this means trusting in yourself and your own abilities. Practise using the skills learned in the body language and first impressions sections in this chapter to ensure that you give the correct message to your investors.

The goal of pitching your business is to get investors to believe and trust in you, your business and the success of your product, services or projects, so that going forward they will invest. Whilst you need to have a profitable business case, people will invest in people; therefore, you need to show that you believe in yourself and that you are committed to doing everything you can to make your business venture a success. Any uncertainty or a sense that you are not completely committed will be evident.

For example, if you are an investor, you would not want to invest in a property project pitched by someone who comes across as visibly nervous, with their head down. However, you may be persuaded to invest by someone who is at ease with themself, has good posture, holds their head high and speaks clearly to you.

The same is true for figure skating. It is fascinating that head up and good posture has been transferrable to interacting and presenting to others. Presentation is key for both sport and business. Whilst belief and confidence help you win a competition in sport, in business, they help you win customers, trust and investment.

Go to Exercise #6 in this chapter to get preparation and guidance on how you can deliver a confident pitch to potential investors.

Self-Confidence from Sport to Business

Just before we move on to self-worth, I'd like to take the time to talk about the parallels from sport to business regarding self-confidence. You may have come across the phrase 'you have to believe to achieve' before. I've heard this said by entrepreneurs, during workout videos and as a sports coach, I've said this to many young athletes. Research has also shown that self-confidence and belief are vital in sport and whilst we can learn a lot from the world of sport, it's also important for business or in fact anything we want to do well at in life. A study by Woodman and Hardy 2003 found that self-confidence can affect performance by approximately 24%. That is a big impact on our ability to perform and just highlights how important it is for us to build our self-confidence. Having belief in our abilities helps us perform in the outside world and achieve our version of success as an entrepreneur.

Self-Worth

Although not exactly the same, the fuel for high self-worth is, in fact, self-confidence. People often think that self-confidence and self-worth are the same; however, from my research, they are slightly different. Self-confidence is about your ability to trust yourself, and self-worth, often referred to as self-esteem, is how you value yourself. This means that you can be just as confident that your self-worth is low as you can be that it is high.

What Exactly is Self-Worth?

Definition

Self-worth: confidence in one's own worth or abilities;
self-respect.

Self-worth is our internal state that is based on how much we understand ourselves, accept and love ourselves. It's basically how much you value yourself despite what others may think or say about you.

Psychologists often use self-worth to describe how you feel about yourself. Those who have negative thoughts about who they are have low self-worth, and those who feel good about themselves have high self-worth. If you say, "I'm a bad person", "I believe in myself", "I'm not good enough", or "I like the way I am", you are referring to your self-worth.

For me, self-worth is related to how much confidence I have in my own ability and how much I value that. In figure skating, I needed to believe in my ability, that I was good enough and that I can execute a double toe loop! Equally, as a person, it is important to like yourself for who you are, as the things that you tell yourself feed into each day of your life. Self-worth is so important because it influences how you feel, and the choices and decisions you make every day. Moreover, it affects how you treat yourself and other people.

As a figure skater, I used affirmations frequently and learnt to appreciate compliments to help raise my self-worth and belief in my ability. Here are my top three ways to increase your self-worth, learnt from sport, that can be applied to your business:

1. Use positive affirmations such as, "I am successful!"

2.   Learn to accept compliments - if someone says, "What a great achievement, well done!" Learn to smile and say, "Thank you!"

3.   Eliminate self-criticism and introduce self-compassion - what could you say instead?

Go to Exercise #7 for some self-worth affirmation guidance.

1.   **"I am successful!"**

How you talk to yourself about your business will determine what you achieve. Yes, that includes the voice in your head. Some affirmations include, "I have the ability to invest in property" and "I will overcome challenges to succeed in my business."

When you believe in your abilities, you value them. For example, suppose you think that you can be a property entrepreneur. In that case, you will have the confidence to negotiate well for deals, decline any projects that do not serve you, have clarity on the next steps in your property journey and proactively seek out financial opportunities and education. All of these actions will support your growth in business and will ultimately lead to an increase in your success. This occurs because you believe in yourself, value yourself and have confidence in your abilities. Go to Exercise #9 for some state of mind affirmations to add to your day!

2.   **"What a great achievement, well done!"**

What did you reply recently when someone gave you a compliment? Did you direct the attention away? Perhaps return the compliment with a compliment? Or did you just accept it? "That's very kind of you, thank you, I appreciate it!" Learning to just accept a lovely comment and understanding that you are actually being grateful by acknowledging the other person's compliment humbly, is great for lifting your self-worth. Not only are you valuing their compliment, but at the same time you are appreciating something good about yourself that will increase your self-worth. If this is something you struggle with, then next time someone gives you a well-deserved compliment, try accepting it and see how it makes you feel.

As a figure skater, people would often compliment me on performances and, of course, my sparkly dresses! I would often thank them and let them know that it meant a lot to me. Which it did! I put a lot of time and effort into my sport and so a compliment was always well received. Accepting the compliment was accepting my hard work had paid off and as a result I performed well. The same is true for business. If you spend many hours working on a product, project or service and someone gives you a compliment on that hard work, then that's a compliment on all the value you've added and a job well done.

3. **Be kind to yourself—What could you say instead?**
As we have mentioned before, life and business doesn't always go to plan. I would have a bad day on the ice and now sometimes I have a bad day in the 'off-ice', as it were. The key here is to be kind to yourself when things go wrong, you have a bad day or make a mistake. Sometimes it's easier to criticise yourself instead, which doesn't help your self-worth or help you move forward. Often, we only see what went wrong, rather than looking for the positives and what this taught us. I have found that taking a step back, accepting the mistake and then asking questions in a compassionate way

helps us learn and feel better about ourselves. Asking yourself, "What would you say about what happened?" and "What could we learn for a more positive outcome next time?" is a more compassionate approach that offers a little kindness. It also helps you think about how you could use a positive attribute next time in a similar situation. As you may recognise, you are adopting a growth state of mind (Dweck) as mentioned at the start of the book.

Be kind to yourself and complete Exercise #8. You can use this exercise any time you need some kindness. Taking the time to write down all your positive attributes, combined with state of mind affirmations, should help you to be your best self and to value yourself for who you are.

Confidence and Money!

In the next section of this chapter, we will discuss your confidence about money, as I feel this is key in business and I've certainly had a money state of mind shift in my property investing business. From studying successful entrepreneurs, I have found them all to have mastered their money state of mind, so this leads on to how we can model this behaviour to get our own financial success. Once again, a money state of mind can be learnt, and this is a quality that I have adopted as an entrepreneur. By having a growth state of mind approach, from sport, I knew I would be able to grow my state of mind around money.

In business and life, money is a key part of our journey and therefore having a confident money state of mind is important to the financial success of our business. What I often hear from people who would like to be an entrepreneur or a property investor is, "I'd love to be a property investor, but I don't have the money" or "I'd love to set up my own business doing x, but I don't have the start-up capital." Do you find yourself saying something similar? If so, this is what I am going to talk about next: your relationship with money. How does confidence affect our attitude towards money? This is how we treat it, respect its worth and most importantly, how we invest it. Do we value it? This is about developing your money state of mind to help you work with money more positively, so you achieve your success in business without your thoughts about money holding you back.

Money State of Mind

Your feelings around money will affect how you handle your money. Here is an example:

Let's say that you don't believe that you can manage money. If you believe this, then the likelihood is that you do not believe you can be financially independent or achieve your version of financial success. This, in turn, can mean that you may not make the correct choices and decisions that will help you be financially successful such as respecting, saving or investing money. By working on your beliefs, you can start to behave in ways that benefit you and help you be successful financially.

As most business ventures often need some capital investment at the start, which is ultimately money, it's worth looking at your belief about money—your money state of mind—to see how this relates to trusting yourself with money and the ability to manage money. You certainly need to have a good relationship with money, and value and respect it to be successful in any business and, in my case, property investing. The conversations that you have with yourself about you and money are therefore very important.

How you value money and what you believe about money often comes from childhood. What your parents would say and what they taught you. Think back to your childhood. Did you hear comments like, "There is more to life than money" or perhaps, "Money doesn't grow on trees." Understanding more about your money state of mind and the beliefs you have today involves going to those underlying beliefs you were taught as a child. Let's look at this more closely by answering the following questions:

1. What was your family attitude towards money?
2. What did you say about people who had money?
3. What does your inner self say about money?

Identifying your money state of mind helps you understand how your deep-rooted beliefs about money were formed and what underlying beliefs you may still have now. I do remember a quote from childhood: 'money doesn't grow on trees'. So, I have grown my positive money state of mind later in life. However, because I was familiar with positive affirmations that I used as a figure skater, I was able to transfer this directly to develop my money state of mind. Affirmations can seem a bit 'la la', I get it, but from my experience, they do work really well and should give you some great results.

So rather than money growing on trees, how can we grow our money state of mind?

Money State of Mind - Scarcity and Abundance

You may be aware, as these are widely spoken about, that there are two money states of mind, scarcity and abundance. As business owners, we are keen to develop an abundance state. Take time to consider what your current beliefs are as a starting point:

1. **Scarcity** – the belief there is never enough. This can mean being afraid to spend money or trying to spend everything with the idea that 'when it's gone, it's gone' and that there is never enough. 'Money doesn't grow on trees.' When you focus on this way of thinking about money, this comes from a place of fear, fear that there is not enough. This, in turn, brings about more scarcity.

2. **Abundance** – believing there will always be enough when you need it. This is about being grateful for what you have right now and for what money may come in the future. By focusing on this state of mind, you bring about more confidence in money, your financial position, as well as the opportunities that may arise to learn more about money, so you have more in the long term.

Focusing on abundance helps us in business, as we believe that we will have enough money to fund our deals, projects, products and make money from our businesses. To fuel an abundant state of mind, we can do some exercises and affirmations that will help us make more positive choices with money, value and respect it, believe there is enough for what we want to do, be grateful for what we currently have and for what we will receive in the future.

Now go to Exercise #10 in this chapter. If you feel that you are more in the scarcity state of mind, these exercises and affirmations will really help you to transition into abundance. However, even if you have a more abundant state of mind, which is great news, these exercises will help you to further increase your abundant state.

Closing Thoughts on Confidence

This chapter and the exercises within it can really help increase your self-confidence and self-worth so that you believe in yourself and value yourself enough to be successful. Having belief in yourself, your abilities and overcoming your limiting beliefs around money should help you be a more confident entrepreneur, pitch more confidently, value yourself to have a better relationship with money, and adopt an abundance money state of mind. Please do ensure you do all the exercises and remember to trust in your abilities. You are enough as a person and you will have enough money when you need it.

Closing Quotes

"Once we believe in ourselves, we can risk curiosity, wonder, spontaneous delight, or any experience that reveals the human spirit."

E.E. Cummings

"Everything I need to make money is showing up at no cost to me."

Jack Canfield

One of my favourites from Henry Ford:

"Whether you think you can or whether you think you can't, you're right."

Exercises: Principle #7

Exercise #1: Facing Your Fears

The best way to deal with things that you fear or that are out of your comfort zone is to face them. Facing your fears helps you build confidence in your abilities and allows you to realise that you can not only overcome your fears, but also any challenges that come your way.

List below five things that you would like to achieve that you fear or are out of your comfort zone. They can be big or small and don't have to be related to business. However, I suggest you have one that is.

1.

2.

3.

4.

5.

Choose one item from the list:

_____

_____

Add a date that you would like to complete this:

_____

_____

List out the first step to achieve this:

_____

_____

_____

_____

_____

Now list all the steps to achieve this:

1. _____
2. _____
3. _____
4. _____
5. _____

You can repeat this with the other items on your list and when you reach the end of these, then you can add more. Sometimes when you set a date and take the first step, getting out of your comfort zone doesn't seem so bad after all. Ensure you reward yourself for overcoming your fear!

Exercise #2: Personal SWOT Analysis

Complete the personal SWOT analysis below to identify your strengths, weaknesses, opportunities and threats. Then write out an action plan to work on the areas where you have weaknesses and use strengths and opportunities to move you forward.

Be as objective as possible when completing these quadrants.

Strengths	Weaknesses
What is it that you do well?	What could you improve on?
What is unique about you?	Where do you lack resources?
What would others say your strengths are?	What would others say your weaknesses are?
What do you enjoy?	What do you dislike?
What are your achievements?	What do you fear?
What skills do you have?	
Opportunities	**Threats**
Could you turn strengths into opportunities?	Who is your competition?
What opportunities do you have right now?	What is your competition doing?
What market trends could you take advantage of?	Are there threats that could be harmful to you?
What problems could you solve?	What threats do your weaknesses expose?

Fill out your own SWOT analysis using the template below:

Strengths	**Weaknesses**
Opportunities	**Threats**

Exercise #3: Action Plan

Time to take action!

Now, let's make a plan that will take advantage of your strengths and seize opportunities whilst minimising any weaknesses or threats. Your action plan should provide clarity and direction for your business so that you can take your path to be successful.

Personal SWOT and Goals

How do your goals align with your SWOT?

_____

_____

How do your goals take advantage of your strengths and opportunities?

_____

_____

What can you do to overcome weaknesses?

_____

_____

List the actions involved (training, outsource, etc.).

_____

_____

_____

_____

How will you mitigate any threats?

_____

_____

Exercise #4: Ten Things Achievement List

List the ten things you are most proud of in your life in an achievement list below. Perhaps you won a medal in a sport, won a competition, you achieved a certification in education, overcame something that you feared, played a key role in an important project, or did you do something kind or charitable that made a positive difference in someone else's life?

1. _____

2. _____

3. _____

4. _____

5. _____

6. _____

7. _____

8. _____

9. _____

10. _____

Exercise #5: Personal Brand Exercise... Who Am I?

In this exercise we will divide the 'who am I?' question into four main components: passion, superpower, values and purpose.

1. **Passion**

What are your passions?

List them here, e.g. figure skating, property, fitness, mindset.

_____

_____

_____

_____

_____

2. **Superpower**

What is your superpower?

e.g. ice-skating, visualisation.

_____

_____

_____

_____

_____

3. **Values**

What is it that makes you angry? What do you care about?

e.g. animal cruelty, lack of ethics.

_____

_____

_____

_____

_____

4. **Purpose**

Where do you think you can make a difference?

e.g. charity, helping others.

_____

_____

_____

_____

_____

Exercise #6: Preparing for an Investor Pitch

There is no magic formula but following this guidance can help you develop a confident pitch:

1. **Start by introducing yourself.**

   People invest in people or a team of people who are behind the business.

   Talk about your experience.

   If this is your first time, then mention previous experience that is relevant.

_____

_____

_____

_____

_____

2. **The opportunity.**

The commercial opportunity: what are you trying to achieve and what value will the project bring in terms of return on investment and/or cashflow?

- What is the opportunity?
- Why is the opportunity worthwhile?
- What's happening in the current market?

_____

_____

_____

_____

_____

3. **Numbers.**

Sometimes an opportunity can be complex for investors who are not so familiar with your business, therefore it's important to remember that numbers are a universal language. Using data will help explain the business case clearly. Remember to be succinct and tell a complete story of the business or project.

_____

_____

_____

_____

_____

4. **Presentation and body language – pitch and practise.**

   Investors are looking at you just as much as your business. They're looking for people who can and will achieve. The confident delivery of your presentation is key and also demonstrates how well you perform when under pressure. As mentioned earlier, someone who is visibly nervous can turn an investor off. If you know you are not able to talk freely, ensure that you prepare a presentation that does some of the explaining for you to help you speak around points more easily with visuals where possible. Practise over and over again out loud at home, so you know your information, numbers and business well. By preparing fully, you will gain more self-confidence and belief. Practise, practise, practise purposefully to be excellent, as per sport.

5. **Connecting with people.**

   A well-prepared, visually attractive presentation that clearly states the investment opportunity is really important. This also reflects the type of person you are. Your manner, what you say and how you say it will also be very clear to the investor. This is something that is very difficult to fake. Be honest about who you are and the opportunity you are presenting as investors are looking for integrity. By focusing on the self-confidence and belief you built in the previous exercises, you'll improve your outward confidence so that you present your authentic true self in the best way possible.

Exercise #7: Personal Self-Worth — Understanding, Love and Respect

Understanding, accepting, and loving yourself will mean that you will no longer require others to accept you, depend on them, or need accomplishments to feel self-worth. Basically, you will not need external factors to feel worthy as you have this internally. When you get to this point though, it's so important to acknowledge the work it took to get there and continue to maintain self-worth with understanding, acceptance and love.

In order to acknowledge self-worth, remember:

1. Whatever people say or do, or anything that happens externally to you, you are in control of how you feel.
   How did you feel last time someone said something negative about you or to you?

   _____

   _____

   _____

   _____

   _____

   Did this affect the rest of your day? (Highlight/circle)

   YES/NO

2. You don't need to please other people.

Do you do things just to please people? (Highlight/circle)

YES/NO

What can you do that will please you?

_____

_____

_____

_____

_____

3. You can choose how you respond to situations and events that happen in your life. In these situations, use your internal resources that represent your authentic self and your true values. Your value comes from the internal measure that you decide.

    Think of an event that happened recently. Did you respond emotionally to this situation?

_____

_____

_____

_____

How can you choose to respond differently?

_____

_____

_____

_____

Below are 12 affirmations to help you with self-worth for acceptance, respect, and love for yourself.

1. I believe in myself.
2. I am happy to be me.
3. I can deal with rejection.
4. I acknowledge my successes and learn from my mistakes.
5. I'm not afraid to make mistakes.
6. I love myself just as I am.
7. I am really proud of all my accomplishments in life.
8. I am a good problem solver.
9. I enjoy trying new things.
10. I respect and value myself.
11. Compliments feel good and I am thankful for them.
12. I like the way I am and how I look.

Exercise #8: Be Kind to Yourself

List your top five positive attributes that you can refer to any time you need to:

1. _____

_____

2. _____

_____

3. _____

_____

4. _____

_____

5. _____

_____

From a self-worth perspective, reflect on something that didn't go your way or a mistake you made, and ask yourself these questions:

- What would you say about what happened?

_____

_____

_____

_____

_____

- What did you learn?

_____

_____

_____

_____

_____

- What positive attributes (from above) do you have that you could apply in a similar situation?

_____

_____

_____

_____

_____

Exercise #9: Three State of Mind Affirmations

1. I have the ability to start and scale my own business.

2. I will overcome all challenges to succeed as an entrepreneur.

3. I release all negative thoughts about entrepreneurship and visualise my TOP goal.

Exercise #10: Three Money State of Mind Affirmations

1. I make positive decisions about what I will do with my money.

2. I create all the money I need so that I can accomplish anything I want to do.

3. I release all negative thoughts about money and visualise my TOP goal and vision.

Ask yourself these questions about what you choose to do with your money:

- What are your spending habits?

_____

_____

_____

_____

_____

- How can you make more money?

_____

_____

_____

_____

_____

- How can you spend less money?

_____

_____

_____

_____

_____

CHAPTER TWELVE

———

PRINCIPLE #8: IT'S NOT EASY, BUT IT IS DOABLE

What Does 'It's Not Easy, But It Is Doable' Mean?

There is no dictionary or common definition for this principle, but it is still equally important. Sport isn't easy, and neither is starting and growing your own business. However, it's not rocket science either; both sport and entrepreneurship are achievable and certainly doable with continued, focused effort over time.

When we first start, we can sometimes think there is a lot to learn, and there is. We can think, can I do it? Is it achievable? Will it be too difficult? What if I fail? In figure skating, for the last question, it would be, 'What if I fall?' and the answer would be to get back up and carry on.

I've found that in figure skating and property entrepreneurship, there are three main points where we may feel that what we would like to achieve

185

seems impossible:

1. At the beginning, when there is a lot to learn.

2. When we need to step out of our comfort zone.

3. When we experience setbacks or challenges.

The Beginning

When starting a new venture, there is always a lot to learn. Everyone must start at the beginning and take the time to learn and understand. When I first started figure skating, and I saw other skaters jumping and spinning, I felt inspired to do the same, but also overwhelmed, as I knew it wasn't going to be easy. However, step by step, I learned to do what they were doing.

When you are starting in business, it's important to remember that setting up and running a business isn't easy, but it is possible by focusing on your reason why, the plan that has been set out, your goals, and the process steps to follow. Then, by putting one foot in front of the other, you get closer to your goal with each step. Making a start is the big first step that brings you closer to your successful outcome and is often the hardest step to take.

> ## Tip #20: By putting one foot in front of the other, we get closer to our goal.

Setbacks and Challenges

Practice in figure skating is similar to the process leading up to a house completion. Once all the practice has been completed, it's time to perform or complete the project. The feeling when I stepped onto the ice to perform in a competition was the same feeling after I completed on an investment project and stepped into it for the first time. I would have a competition 'quiver' when I was waiting on the ice, ready to start. I would also have an after-sale 'worry' when I had just bought a house, and all the renovation work still needed to be done. I would look at a room and see that I'd paid £xxx for a house, and it was a mess, damp and dark, with a lot of work to complete. This was when we would start the renovations, the all-important transformation. With figure skating, all the hard work was done leading up to the competition, but this was the time that I stood on the ice, ready to start my performance in a competition that really mattered. What I did in the next 3-4 minutes on the ice was important. At the same time, it was also the opportunity to enjoy the performance, like enjoying the property renovation journey. This is where state of mind is so crucial to success.

What happens if things don't go to plan? What if there is an issue on a project, a business challenge? In skating, what if I fell over? Well, on the ice, I was taught to get up, carry on as usual and reflect after. The same is true when problems occur in business. It's essential to keep going. Sometimes this can be easier said than done, and at times if I had a lousy skating performance, I would want to give up. I never did, and I have taken this learning forward into my property business. Although there are times where quick 'on the spot' firefighting is required, mainly in the business world, you have time to think and refocus to carry on. There are some visualisation and relaxation exercises at the end of this chapter to help you realise that this is not always easy, that challenges occur, and how you can calm down and carry on.

The Comfort Zone

We also naturally fear the unknown. Above, I likened my first property investment to my first skating competition. When getting out of your comfort zone, learning, and growing, there is an anxiety that comes with it. Sometimes if we find ourselves in difficult unfamiliar situations, we feel flustered and apprehensive, which is a perfectly natural response to what we perceive as a threatening situation. There is a worry that things might not go well. In figure skating, this was a common situation that I repeatedly experienced in competitions, tests, and shows. As an entrepreneur, we may face this when doing our first project, talking to the customer for the first time or presenting to an investor. It may not be easy, but we need to take these first steps to start so that we can then get better and move forward. We gain more confidence by doing more, but most of us still get anxious. That's normal, and it's how we deal with these emotions that make the difference.

When you are being put under pressure to perform, you feel more threatened. As you perceive a threat, this causes you to contract your muscles, have involuntarily dilated or enlarged pupils, and release adrenaline. This is what is commonly known as the 'fight or flight' response. The fight or flight response is a survival mechanism that enables us to react quickly to life-threatening situations. The almost instantaneous succession of hormonal changes and physiological responses helps us fight off an impending threat or flee to safety. However, as we have not evolved to deal with modern-day life, the body can overreact to situations that are not life-threatening, such as business pressures, challenges, or being out of our comfort zone. This means that you have a 'fight or flight' reaction because you are aware of the consequences of not performing, not doing well, things going wrong or perhaps not living up to expectations for a client or investor. This is about what can go wrong, and you have a very good idea of what can go wrong!

> # Tip #21: You already have a good idea of what can go wrong, so focus on what will go well.

Instead of triggering this response, try reframing this by focusing your attention on what will go well. The positive aspect of the performance, project, product, or service. How is your product going to help others and help you? What will the product look like when it's completed? In figure skating, I often used visualisation or mental imagery to 'see' an outcome, and I found this to be a powerful way of performing well.

Similarly, when starting a renovation project, I visualise what the house will look like once we have completed the renovations, taking into account what I see, hear, smell, and feel. It's the first thought I have once I have the after-sale 'worry'. When you do this, your perception then starts to reinforce self-confidence, reassurance, and belief that this is possible, and you can do this. This also helps with self-confidence and belief, as discussed in Chapter Eleven.

Remember that a level of being anxious or nervous is good and helpful. Still, it's when we cannot control this response that it causes problems for us and our business, meaning that we cannot perform to the best of our abilities.

Visualisation for Your TOP Goal Success

Visualisation is also very powerful for thinking about your TOP goal and produces some amazing results. This type of visualisation is more about the overall picture of what you want your life to be like, your TOP goal, and how you see yourself as being successful. What is it that you are doing? What can you see and hear? An excellent way to do this is by visualising yourself being successful as a movie on a screen in front of you and then actually stepping into the movie yourself to experience the successful you. Whether it is giving the best figure skating performance, walking around 20 houses that you own, helping 100 people, being in an office with 10 of your employees enjoying their work; the important point is that you need to know what success looks like for you so you can visualise what it is that you want. The complete exercise for this is at the end of this chapter (Exercise #3) and tells you step by step, the process to use every day as part of your routine. The 'power hour' is the perfect time to do this. It does take time for your subconscious to believe, but it really can work well to give you a fantastic outcome.

Closing Quote

―――――

"Imagery can't make you perform beyond your capabilities, but it can help you reach your potential."

Tom Seabourne, Ph.D.

―――――

Exercises: Principle #8

Visualisation involves mental imagery, or an imaginary rehearsal, using all our senses, and I have found it to be so powerful. I was often asked in figure skating to imagine performing a move and to think about what I was feeling and hearing. Create a mental image that feels like it's happening to you. The key is that it is about what is happening to you, and you are not watching yourself like a movie, you are actually in the movie!

Practising mental imagery or visualisation is a great addition to your routine, so that you can use it to get the results that you desire and also as a fight or flight response. You will not become better at visualisation just by reading this book, you'll need some focused practice so that you can use it when you next feel anxious about a situation, like giving a presentation to an investor.

Exercise #1: Why Visualisation Works

Try this:

1. Think of your favourite meal.
2. Close your eyes and imagine it's on the table in front of you.
3. Imagine how it smells and what it looks like.
4. Imagine you are eating your favourite food. Experience the wonderful taste and texture.
5. Now really take some time and imagine the food as if it's real.

What meal did you imagine?

_____

_____

Even if you were just a little bit hungry, I'm sure now you are probably hungrier and really want your favourite food! This shows you the direct connection between the thoughts you are having and your body's reaction to those thoughts. Mental imagery or visualisation takes advantage of this phenomenon to influence our emotional state of mind to take action.

Now try this for your business:

1. Think of your ideal business (that fits with your vision and TOP goal).

2. Really think about it. Close your eyes and imagine your product or client is right in front of you or you are delivering your service. For property investing, I often imagine the property right in front of me, I'm looking at it from the road opposite, I own it and I have renovated it.

3. Imagine how it looks and touch it. What does it feel like, what can you see, hear and smell? If you have a service, for example, an event, imagine yourself delivering the service: who is there, what do you feel, hear and smell? For property investing, I imagine walking inside the house and seeing the décor, the furniture, and colours.

4. As before, don't just think about it for a few seconds and move on… take the time to imagine it all as if it's real.

What's your ideal business?

_____

_____

What if you are having a business worry? Perhaps, you've signed a contract and although excited, you are worried about the delivery. Try this exercise to focus on the end result and adapt as necessary:

1. Personally, I like to close my eyes and imagine the situation now; your business worry.

2. Think about the outcome. Delivering the service, making peoples' lives easier, people using your product or service.

3. Really think about it. This is all happening right in front of you.

4. What can you see, hear, smell? What are people saying? Who is there? What does it feel like?

5. Once again, don't just think about it for a few seconds and move on… take the time to imagine the situation as if it's real to you.

Here is a property investing example to help you:

I've just bought a house and have an after-sale 'worry'.

1. I walk into the worst room in the house. The most damp and dark one!

2. I close my eyes. Then think what I would like this room to look like once it's been renovated and ready for tenants to move in.

3. Then I imagine I am standing in that room.

4. I imagine how it looks, what the décor is, look at the furniture (sofa, bed, chest of drawers, carpet). What are the colours, what does it feel like, what can I hear and smell? (I often imagine the smell of new furniture.)

5. I really take time to imagine the room as if it's real.

Did that help you focus on the result and what you are trying to achieve? Repeat this as necessary to reinforce what you are going to achieve.

Exercise #2: Visualisation for Relaxation

1. Sit or lie down and then close your eyes.

2.   Think of a place that is peaceful and will calm you. For example, a warm sunny beach.

3.   Imagine yourself being there. Imagine what you would feel, see, hear, taste and smell. For our beach example, it may be the waves splashing into the shore, a salty smell, warm sun on your face, feeling of the sand between your toes.

4.   Set a timer for 5 minutes and allow yourself to get lost. Remember this is to relax yourself.

Exercise #3: The Successful You

Athletes use visualisation as a mental rehearsal. As an example, here is a quote by Wayne Rooney:

―――――――――――

"I lie in bed the night before the game and visualise myself scoring goals or doing well. You're trying to put yourself in that moment and trying to prepare yourself, to have a 'memory' before the game. I've always done it, my whole life."

Wayne Rooney

―――――――――――

Personally, I love a good movie and a chocolate bar, I hope you do too! The exercise below is a movie about the successful you and your favourite chocolate bar. I was taught this exercise by a psychologist when I was a teenager as I personally liked movies and chocolate. In the movie, as a teenager, I would imagine I was doing a successful skating performance at my next test or competition. However, I've since used the same exercise to apply to the successful me, which I will now share below so you can imagine your version of the successful you. So, let's go and create the movie of the successful you and then let's make it feel real!

A good time to do this exercise is in the power hour after meditation.

1. Close your eyes. Think about the successful you, got it? Now think about your favourite chocolate bar.

2. Imagine that you are now at home on your comfy sofa watching a movie on TV and this movie is about the successful you. Imagine what you are doing on the TV screen, what you look like and how well you are doing it. Use as much detail as possible. What do you look like, what can you see, hear, smell, what are others saying, what do you feel, where are you?

3. Now walk over to the TV and imagine yourself stepping into the screen so you are now in the movie. Now experience all of step two, but this time you are actually in the movie experiencing this as yourself. Remember all of the details. What do you look like, what do you see, hear, smell, what are others saying, what are you feeling, where are you?

4. Now step back out of the movie and look back at the TV screen. Shrink the screen down to the size of your favourite chocolate bar and eat it piece by piece. As you put each piece into your mouth, chew and swallow, think of yourself being successful. As the movie of the 'successful you' is being digested, think of this as being absorbed into your mind and body, so it becomes part of you. Once you have finished, then you can open your eyes.

Don't forget, the State Of Mind Playbook has all templates and exercises. It's free to download at: www.stateofmindplaybook.com.

CHAPTER THIRTEEN

—————

PRINCIPLE #9: MOTIVATION

In this chapter, we will explore what motivation is and our motivational states starting with flow. What it is that motivates us, how motivation is linked to our reason why and how this relates to motivational strategies in sport. So, let's start at the very beginning with a definition.

Definition

Motivation: the word motivation is derived from the word 'motive', meaning desires, wants, needs or drives within a person. It is the process of stimulating individuals to create actions to achieve goals.

Flow and TOP Goals

Motivation is key in sport as there are times that you need to keep going and put in the required effort even if you are tired, bored or in pain. You will also need to be motivated to show up for practice when you have the desire to do other fun things, meet friends or go to a party. I remember getting up very early at 4 a.m., sometimes when it was dark and cold, to practice on a freezing cold ice-rink, fall over a fair few times and practise the same move over and over again. Moreover, I would prioritise this over my social life and spending time with friends. However, I never questioned it. Most of the time, I loved to go to the ice-rink, and the more difficult times were worth it to me. I have applied this state of mind to my property investing business. If you are growing your business, then motivation is essential to keep you working consistently in the face of challenges.

The Ultimate Motivational State

Motivation, on a high level, is related to how much we are 'in flow' or sometimes referred to as being 'in the zone' with what we are doing. Flow, as it is commonly known today was termed by the psychologist Mihály Csíkszentmihályi (1975). Being 'in flow' means enjoying a task or activity so much that we are engaged and unaware of anything around us, fully submerged and unaware of time. Flow is the ultimate motivational state where nothing else matters. In this state of flow, self-consciousness is lost and athletes, or anyone for that matter, can just become one with their activity. For me, my skates feel like an extension of my legs whilst I am in flow.

So, what is the key to being in 'flow'? Well, according to Nakamura et al. (2009), if we set unrealistic challenges, this can cause us to worry or feel anxious. However, if we are not challenged enough, this can lead to boredom. So, to promote flow, we need to stretch ourselves a little further each time and step just outside of our comfort zone continuously. We also need to enjoy what we are doing and know why we are doing it.

I think we can all agree, there are times in our life when we feel 'in flow' with what we are doing. I'm sure you can remember a time that you were so engrossed in an activity that you lost track of time? It's likely that this activity was aligned with your reason why, TOP goal and your values. However, why is it that sometimes we are excited and find it easy to get motivated or be in 'flow', yet other times, we procrastinate, and it seems impossible to figure out how to get motivated? Is it just that these tasks are realistically achievable for our current skillset? Or is there something more? Why do some things motivate us and others just don't? This chapter has some great ideas based on insightful research of what motivates us, with some valuable exercises on getting and staying motivated.

Tip #22: Work on your business for the right reasons, because you enjoy it!

What Motivates Us?

We are often motivated by tasks that are fun and either within our comfort zone or just outside it, but there are some 'motives' that require us to do tasks we are not comfortable with. There is often a point, what I like to call a 'tipping point' for these tasks, where we feel the discomfort caused by not doing a task outweighs the discomfort of just doing it. The point where things would start to go wrong or 'fall over' if you didn't complete these tasks. As Steven Pressfield states in "The War of Art" "At some point, the pain of not doing it becomes greater than the pain of doing it."

For example, an athlete would get up on a rainy, cold morning at 5 a.m. to train, rather than not improve, be overtaken by competitors or perhaps perform badly at a competition. All athletes are individuals, meaning that they are motivated in different ways. As per Chapter Five the important point is that we know our personal reasons why and the TOP goal that fuels our desire. Knowing this means that we would rather feel uncomfortable making a call to a vendor keen to sell their house, than feel disappointed that we didn't get the property. If we didn't make the call, perhaps we would miss out on a potential project and an opportunity to make a great return on investment. We would, therefore, rather make the uncomfortable phone call than risk not getting the next property project to help fulfil our TOP goal.

How do we get into 'flow', and what can we do to increase our chances of passing the tipping point?

If we are doing what we love and the activity is aligned with our ability level, then we will be in a state of flow most of the time. That is how we know we are doing tasks and filling our days with what really matters to us. Experiencing flow intrinsically motivates us, meaning that enjoyment motivates us, so it is important to engage in enjoyable activities that are conducive to it. We want to be in flow most of the time, but I think we can all agree that even if we know our reasons why, the simple fact is that there are tasks that we simply do not like doing. That's life, and if we accept this, but know overall that we love what we are doing, and we know why we are doing it, we start to focus our attention back on the vision board, and this helps push us forward. I believe that 80% logic applies here, 80% in flow and 20% just do it tasks! So basically, this is about accepting that no matter how much we may love what we are doing overall, there will be some tasks we need to just get done to fulfil our reason why that we will not feel motivated to do. Sometimes starting these tasks can be the most challenging step to overcome, even if you have a reason why and you really want to do it. Therefore, I will outline a few key steps that will help you get motivated if something is outside of your fun flow state. This will enable you to take those difficult steps that are part of the process to achieve what's on your vision board and aligned to your values.

Key motivational steps to help you get those 20% of 'just do it!' tasks done:

1. Firstly, if you are starting a new business venture and assuming you have your desire and reason why then the next step is to actually make a start! Taking action is often a big step, but this is fundamental to getting motivated, although this can be the hardest step to take. I found out a surprising fact from James Clear, Motivation: The Scientific Guide on How to Get and Stay Motivated, that motivation often comes after starting a new behaviour rather than before—the result of taking action rather than its cause. Getting started by taking small steps will begin to inspire you, and that will create momentum, making it easier to keep going. I recommend a business plan as per Chapter Seven to get started. Your business plan will act as a 'blueprint' of your business and make you think about your market, financials, and competitors, as well as goals and targets. Chapter Seven, Principle #3: Routine has a business plan guide, so you should have completed this already. If not, please do complete your business plan now. Chapter Seven also gives a unique approach to routine with multiple levels of planning, from a business plan to daily routines, that help form habits.

2. We have mentioned this A LOT and covered this in Chapter Five, but having a strong reason why that will trigger your 'motive' to take action is very important. This is key to getting motivated. Ensure the vision board that you created is visible for you to look at every day to remind you of your reason why. This will vary for different people, but knowing the reason why you are doing something will motivate you to do it. For example, if you would like to lose weight to be in great shape for a trip of a lifetime holiday, you have your reason why you will make it through the 5k run or the tough circuit training work out at 6:30 a.m. in the morning. However, ensure you remind yourself of this regularly so that you do not lose focus or quit when you have a tough day. You will then have the motivation to keep going, because your 'why' is clear and is there in front of you every day.

Tip #23: If you haven't done so already, put your vision board in a place you can see it every day. This will continually remind you of your reason why so you are always motivated to take action.

---

3. Set SMART goals. We covered this in Chapter Six about setting SMART (Specific, Measurable, Achievable, Realistic, Timebound) goals. When you set goals, you decide to act in a way to achieve what you want. Set correctly, goals give you direction to focus on a measurable endpoint. Ensure you break up your goals into

manageable tasks. Try telling someone about your goals to make you accountable. This way, you will be more motivated as you would rather not have to explain why you didn't take any action!

4. 'Do what you love, love what you do!' Athletes overall do love their sport. I know I did (most of the time!). I would often be in a state of flow on the ice, oblivious of my surroundings and the time passing. I would often describe it as being lost in the moment, but it was often more than a moment. The same applies to your business if you love it. I can lose myself doing property tasks too, some of my favourites are sourcing properties and working out a business case. Another favourite time is visiting the house at the end of the project. I usually stand in the same place before and after the renovations to take a photo so that I can see the transformation. I can easily lose an afternoon putting the final touches on renovations and taking in what we have achieved within the space. Remembering what you love and reflecting on these moments can help you get the 'just do it' tasks done, especially if you can then move on to the things you love doing after. What more motivation do you need?

5. Automate your behaviour by setting a schedule for yourself. Decision-making on autopilot gives your goals a time and place, making you more likely to follow through regardless of your motivation levels. See Chapter Seven, Principle #3: Routine. This will really help you to 'eat your vegetables' as you know they are good for you, getting those difficult tasks done, knowing that you will be closer to your vision and TOP goal.

Many of the steps above to get motivated are covered earlier in this book, so if you complete all the exercises and tasks in each chapter, then you should see your motivation levels increase as a result.

Motivation in Sport

In sport, psychologists widely research and discuss two types of motivation: intrinsic and extrinsic.

1. Intrinsic motivation is the behaviour driven internally by meaningful rewards such as enjoyment, challenge, competing, and learning a new skill. The focus is concentrating on skill improvement to grow as an athlete. This is about being 'in flow'.

2. Extrinsic motivation is about getting rewards and avoiding any negative consequences. Rewards can be winning cups and medals or perhaps a scholarship. Avoiding negative consequences can be not making the team for an event, disappointing supportive parents or letting them down. There is a focus here on the outcome of athletic competitions or goals.

Balancing Intrinsic and Extrinsic

Intrinsic motivation helps athletes focus more in the present, helping to maintain a consistent level through the process of training. For entrepreneurship, this would be more about building a business. In this case, you are more focused during the everyday 'practice', become more confident and enjoy your work more.

Extrinsic rewards are a very fundamental component in competitive sport and, of course, can be applied to business. What if a British figure skater did not have Team GB to aim for? If scholarships were not offered anymore by colleges? Bursaries at universities? No business awards for being great in your field? If used correctly, these rewards can be beneficial. However, overuse of extrinsic rewards can have the opposite effect by negatively affecting performance, which can lead to demotivation.

If extrinsic motivation is more dominant, we experience a greater level of competitive pressure; comparison, devaluing self-worth, anxiety, and an inability to deal with failure. When this happens, your sport or your business can feel like 'hard work'.

There may be athletes with one strategy or the other, or perhaps one more dominant or even a mix. However, ideally, I believe a balance that is best suited to us as individuals would serve us well, so that we have intrinsic motivation to be in flow with our tasks and extrinsic, so we are motivated to achieve. We want to be in the ultimate flow state when working in our business so that we enjoy it and work to improve every day to reach our goals—the extrinsic motivator.

To have the optimal motivation levels, we ideally want to implement an intrinsic motivational strategy to be in flow in our business with a focus on extrinsic motivation to ensure that we work towards our goals and get through challenges because we know why we are showing up.

How to Stay Motivated?

If we assume that you have taken all the steps to get motivated, you are doing what you love, you know your reason why, you have written a business plan, you have plans and routines in place, then what is next? Once we get motivated, how do we stay motivated?

Keeping ourselves motivated is key to achieving our goals, and we can do the following to help stay motivated:

1. Ensure that our vision board is visible every day. This will keep you motivated to push forward. If there are any changes to be made, then review it and update it. If you achieve everything on your vision board, amazing! It's time to create another one. Keep it reviewed, refreshed and updated.

2. Track your progress towards your goal and focus on what you have achieved. Reward yourself for reaching milestones or completing tasks. Do not worry if you need to adjust or change; this is all part of the learning. This was covered in Chapter Eight, Principle #4: Celebrate Success and Learn from Mistakes.

3. Adhere to what is known and detailed in The Goldilocks Rule by James Clear. The Goldilocks Rule states that to have optimal motivation on tasks, the task needs to be a little more difficult than our current abilities but not too difficult, as we will lose motivation because we can't do the task. As humans, we love challenges, but only those that challenge us a step further each time. If tasks fall below your current ability level, they can be boring, and those far beyond may be discouraging. However, those right on the borderline are very motivating to us. It's therefore important that we have a plan to follow that allows us to progress just outside our comfort zone each time, so that we are in flow and stay motivated.

4. Do not do it alone! Find other people doing the same thing or similar to connect with. Go to networking events and support groups. This may be difficult at first but having people to share challenges and discuss ideas with helps inspire us and keeps motivation levels up. I found fellow figure skaters helped me keep

motivated by working with them, meeting up, training together and doing teamwork activities. It's a lot of fun too! Likewise, working with fellow property investors and business owners, networking, sharing ideas, and catching up with like-minded people helps us to move forward more quickly. As per my skating days, it's fun as well. My favourite saying here is 'TEAM – Together Everyone Achieves More'.

Tip #24: Think TEAM - Together Everyone Achieves More.

Motivational Quotes

Here are seven motivational quotes to close this chapter and give you a great state of mind to start the exercises that follow:

"The secret of getting ahead is getting started."

Mark Twain

"It's only after you've stepped outside your comfort zone that you begin to change, grow, and transform."

Roy T. Bennett

"Be thankful for what you have: you'll end up having more. If you concentrate on what you don't have, you will never have enough."

Opera Winfrey

"It always seems impossible until it's done."

Nelson Mandela

"Knowing is not enough; we must apply. Willing is not enough; we must do."

Johann Wolfgang Von Goethe

"Don't worry about failure. Worry about the chances you miss when you don't even try."

Sherman Finesilver

"Success is not an accident; success is a choice."

Stephen Curry

Exercises: Principle #9

Exercise #1

What activities do you enjoy doing? An activity where you are 'in flow' and you lose track of time.

_____

_____

_____

_____

_____

Exercise #2

Remind yourself of your reason why from Chapter Five (use your vision board or use a sentence from your vision board).

_____

_____

_____

_____

_____

Remind yourself of your TOP goal from Chapter Six here:

_____

_____

Exercise #3: Taking Action

Write down your first action if getting started, or your next action.

_____

_____

Is it a flow action or reason why? (circle/highlight)

FLOW / REASON WHY

Imagining you are an entrepreneur, what tasks do you love?

_____

_____

_____

_____

_____

Make it fun... what do you enjoy about your business or business idea?

_____

_____

_____

_____

_____

Exercise #4: Discover Your Strengths (Flow)

We often focus too much time on our weaknesses. Let's change this and focus on strengths. Find somewhere comfortable, close your eyes if possible and take yourself to these moments:

- As a child what games did you like the most?

_____

_____

_____

_____

_____

- What did you imagine yourself as?

_____

_____

_____

_____

_____

- As a child, what activities made you lose track of time?

_____

_____

_____

_____

_____

- As an adult, what activities make you lose track of time?

_____

_____

_____

_____

_____

- What makes your energy increase and what does that say about you?

_____

_____

_____

_____

_____

- As an adult, think of an achievement you are proud of. What were you doing?

_____

_____

_____

_____

_____

- Following on from the previous question, what was its impact on you/the people around you?

_____

_____

_____

_____

_____

- Now write down a list of your strengths.

My strengths:

_____

_____

_____

_____

_____

This exercise makes us look at ourselves, so you understand who you are, and what achievements you are most proud of. Use this exercise when you come face-to-face with new challenges. We all have areas that we need to improve but focusing on our strengths is much more motivating.

CHAPTER FOURTEEN

———

PRINCIPLE #10: DETERMINATION AND GRIT

Determination

During my dad's speech at my wedding, he told all of our guests how much determination I had as a child. Once I made up my mind, there was no doubt in my head what I wanted, and I would pursue this with passion. I believe this sums up determination, but let's take a look at the definition.

> ## Definition
>
> **Determination:** the quality of being determined; firmness of purpose, "those who succeed because of sheer grit and determination."

Yes, I believe that's it! Determination is a firm intent, a decision that has been reached. An example could be wanting to achieve something so much, that you have the strength to keep going, taking a test many times even if you have failed dozens of times before. It is a powerful trait that means you are intent on reaching your goals. The opposite would lead to hesitation, indecisiveness, and generally being disinterested. However, right at the other end of the scale, being too determined to achieve a goal could lead to the inability to see any issues or challenges or being overly obsessed. Once you have firm intent to move forward with a goal and work on your tasks, then as you do so, it is inevitable that you will face challenges along the way. However, if you have learnt the principle of being determined to achieve your goals, you will focus all your efforts consistently, persevering until the task is completed.

As you can see above, to have determination, you also need to have a clear idea of what it is that you want, and you've really got to want it. Basically, a TOP goal where you understand exactly why you want to achieve it. For me, I always wanted to be the best I could be. To achieve and be successful in figure skating, to attain the highest standard and become a professional figure skater and coach. I am determined in everything I do and going forward, this is still true. I always want to show up as my best self in whatever I do. I am constantly committed and determined to achieve this in my business and set myself targets that align with this.

In the first principle, you completed your goals, reason, desire and what success means to you, so you know what you want, why you want it and have something to be determined about. Take a moment to think about these.

Look at your vision board…

What is your TOP goal?

What is your reason why?

What does success mean to you?

Were you able to answer the questions above without looking back at the previous chapters? If you were not able to, take some extra time now to ensure you can next time, or at least by the end of reading this book.

Tip #25: Know your TOP goal, your reason why and what success means to you to help you be more determined.

Now you are very clear on your TOP goal, reason, and success, you are ready to understand more of what it means to be determined. How to keep going and not give up, and the benefits you will get from being more determined.

The Benefit of Being Determined; Why Is It Important?

One major benefit of being determined, is that you achieve what you set out to do. If this is a TOP goal, then you will reap the benefits of this achievement. There is also a level of satisfaction that comes with achieving a TOP goal that will make you feel confident and like a champion. Would you like to have these benefits? Read on to understand how you can be more determined…

How Can You Be Determined?

Let us start by thinking about what your behaviour will be if you are not determined. You will often give up and not get things completed. However, if you are determined to achieve a worthwhile goal, you will reap the rewards, including being more confident and more motivated.

An example might be that a young person may be determined to graduate from university and get a bachelor's degree despite financial hardships. Or a baseball player who is determined to catch a ball that seems to have been hit too far away. The player would try his best to catch the ball instead of giving up. In my experience, I may be determined to continue with a routine despite feeling tired and will be determined to make it to the end of the routine instead of giving up, even if it is a struggle. Sometimes, if a jump wasn't perfect in the air, I would be able to rescue it on the landing. In property investing, it could mean being determined to keep going to obtain planning permission despite having pushbacks and needing to change our plans several times, but not giving up.

A determined person will try all options, if possible, to achieve a goal. There are instances, of course, where some things can be judged to be out of our reach. The baseball player, for example, would be ill-advised to run after a ball that was hit out of the ballpark. So, it's worth being realistic about your business goals, ensure that you are making your goals SMART and just outside your comfort zone, so you stay within your flow. Otherwise, this could lead to unnecessary disappointment, lack of motivation and determination just because you were unrealistic about your goal attainment and your current skill level.

To be determined, you need to keep focused on your worthy SMART goals. To keep going, not give in to distractions, be committed and stay true to your values. Let's explore each of these further.

1. **Keep Going:** it's worth remembering that most people give up too soon on their business journey. A person may have a goal to have a portfolio of twenty houses. However, when the task of buying and renovating houses seems more difficult than they thought, that person may weigh up the desire to achieve their property goal, versus the work required and decide that is it easier to quit. For example, investing in property takes time, knowledge, and money, so it may be easier in the short term for some to continue to work in their 9-5 job instead, rather than put in the additional work to achieve a TOP goal. In some circumstances, this person may not have the confidence in their ability to be able to complete a given task or achieve their goal. An example of this could be a young aspiring actor who would like a lead role on Broadway but feels there is too much competition and they would not be good enough, so they decide not to pursue this career.

I'm sure you have met people that jump from one thing to another and never complete what they started. This can be due to the fact that these people lack focus and determination, their reason why may not be strong and they may not have a firm purpose to stay with their plan and achieve their goal.

> # Tip #26: Keep on achieving your business goals even when it's difficult and you face challenges.

2. **Be committed:** being committed to your goals and your journey means making a well thought through plan. One that describes the best steps to take to achieve your goals and then sticking firmly with that plan without deviation. Unless, of course, you plan in that deviation due to circumstances changing.

   This can prove difficult at times, but it is a necessity if you truly want to become great at what you do. Be determined to push yourself just a little bit further and make choices that help you become better. For example watch a documentary, read a book or listen to a podcast, rather than watching a series or movies on TV. The key is to ensure that your life revolves around your TOP goal, reason, and desire.

3. **Avoid distractions:** this is something to watch out for! At the end of this chapter, there is an exercise to help you avoid distractions, as they really hinder productivity. Modern-day phone alerts and emails can be a big distraction! Navigating the road to being an entrepreneur does not come easy, and you may find several obstacles in your way. Sometimes it may feel that you are struggling a lot to make a small impact. You may have friends who want to go

out for dinner and may be offended when you decline their kind offer. However, remember that the journey to owning a successful, thriving business isn't always easy. Therefore, it is important to socialise on your own terms and schedule, not someone else's. The simple fact is that if you do not take time to focus and work on your goals, then no one else will. Each distraction will mean that you could miss an opportunity, such as attending a meeting or going to a networking event. As an analogy, I often think of distractions as weeds in a well-maintained garden. They soak up nutrients, inhibit a plants growth and spoil the look of a beautiful garden. Now, if you have real friends, they will completely understand your situation and what you are trying to achieve, so it is really important to keep these people in your life. I have a few good friends whom I spend my time with who support and help me, and these really are my true friends.

4. **Narrow down your choices:** it is impossible to try to do everything at once, and as the saying goes, you can be a 'Jack of all trades and a master of none.' Choose goals and tasks that resonate with your reason why and those that make your 'boat go faster.' It is impossible to grow a successful, profitable business overnight. Instead, focus your work on the next deal, product, service or project. Also, ensure that what you decide to work on meets your business case, business plan, and aligns with what you want to achieve, along with your goals and vision.

As per point three, you'll also want to remove your distractions. If you do not eliminate your distractions, they will lead to a lack of focus, and you won't know what to do even if you know what is best. However, if you take time to find out what distracts you and stay committed to avoiding those distractions, you'll become a lot more focused on your goals.

With fewer choices to make, your mind will have fewer excuses for not taking a course, making a journey or committing to work.

5. **Be true to your values:** you identified your values at the start of this book. Take time to read them again now, and every day, to make sure you are clear and edit them if you need to. Your values should guide you each step of the way in your business so that you do not make a compromise for anything or anyone. It is really important to be clear on your values to be true to yourself, who you are and what you want to achieve. This is so important to your success. Your values give you a purpose for staying committed to your goals even if, at times, things may seem hopeless or meaningless.

   This is also one of the factors in being happy. If you stay true to yourself to get ahead regardless of your position, then you will be able to sleep at night and live a happier, healthier life. Keep your values somewhere you can see them every day, so that you remain aligned with them and work towards them proactively.

6. **Align, pivot and adapt your actions regularly:** most people find it difficult to break routines and habits they are used to, whether these serve them well or not, especially if these were aligned to initial beliefs. However, life does change, and if the current tasks you are doing are not aligned with your new direction, e.g. success in your business, then changes will need to be made. If your actions do not serve you well, then you need to change them.

   Being open to change and being able to adapt and pivot is

important. It is worth noting that the road you are travelling on may also change in direction, so you may fancy taking a detour on the way, meaning that your goals and the route you are taking to achieve them may change as well. Something may happen beyond your control that may mean that you wish to change how you deliver your product or service, where you invest or use another strategy. As a result, you will need to update your goals, methods, plans and road maps to keep up with your change in direction. This is ok, plans change, so you must have the flexibility to try new things that might be out of your comfort zone. Just make sure that you have thought through plans to ensure your new direction is the right one for you.

7.   **Take action:** it is one thing knowing what to do, but equally important is to take the action required to get to your goals. Having a vision, as per your vision board, is very important, as is having a plan to get there, with steps outlined towards your goal. You also need to take action to move closer to your desired outcome. I've seen many property investors that have the knowledge to succeed, but who don't take any action.

Ensure you take action on the opportunities that align with your goals and values. Do not wait for inspiration but instead, seek it, and you will find it.

8.   **Remember the end result:** there's a well-known saying by Mike Tyson: "Everybody has a plan until they get punched in the face." This is when your reality sinks in, and you have to deal with the present situation. There are times in business that things do not go to plan, and at those times, you may feel like giving up. It is at these

times that the decision you make will affect what will happen for the rest of your life.

Fortitude, which is basically courage in pain or adversity, is directly linked to grit. All great entrepreneurs have courage, regardless of the situation, and this is paramount to being successful.

Tip #27: Remember, at challenging times, the finish line is within arm's reach!

Grit

That last point leads me nicely on to grit! Let's talk about how grit works with determination. At the start of this chapter, there is a definition of determination that states that people who are determined are 'those who succeed because of sheer grit and determination.' We often hear of the word grit when talking about determination. So, what exactly does grit mean?

What Is Grit?

Grit is about having so much passion for one thing that you're willing to overcome all obstacles in order to achieve it.

Grit is the combination of being persistent, as per Chapter Nine, and having determination. As we have found out in this chapter so far, determination is about firmness of purpose: 'I have decided' whilst being persistent. It is the continuation of action around that purpose, describing the actions you require to move forward. In technical terms, persistence is considered 'steadfastness in doing something despite difficulty or delay in achieving success,' and determination is considered 'firm intention'. When someone perseveres, it is because they see the end goal that they are determined to achieve. Here we can see that both persistence and determination need to come together to form grit in order to get success.

Grit and Your TOP Goal

Achievement of a TOP goal takes a lot of effort, direction and duration. In Malcolm Gladwell's bestselling book Outliers, he states that it is important to have goals combined with lots and lots of practice. He believes that to be a contender 10,000 hours of practise, which equates to 20 hours of effort per week over ten years duration is required in the direction of your TOP goal. However, the point to note here, and this is very clearly explained in Bounce by Matthew Syed, is that this effort has to be purposeful practice. This means that your effort must be focused on your goal and needs to be high-quality practice. That is also where you will need the courage, stamina and grit to keep going.

To apply this to our business, we need to ensure that all of our efforts are consistent and in line with our goals, so that all the work we do is focused, purposeful, meets our values and is directed to what we want to achieve.

What About Courage and Fear of Failure?

We mentioned courage above, which is difficult to measure; however, it is directly proportional to your level of grit and determination. You will need to manage your fear of failure as most people with grit are not afraid to fail and focus more on being a hunter of success. These people know that there are valuable lessons to be learned in the mistakes they make, as mentioned in Chapter Eight, and that this is a required prerequisite of attaining your goals.

What if you are afraid to fail? Well, you are not alone, and millions of people have different manifestations and levels of 'the fear of failure'. The question is, what about if you face fear daily? As per Eleanor Roosevelt, "Do something every day that scares you." To grow our courage, we can exercise it regularly, daily if possible, similar to exercising a muscle. If you do not do something often that scares you or pushes you out of your comfort zone, then similar to a muscle that is not exercised, it will lessen. Courage helps us fuel the 'grit fire' and feed off each action to keep our fire burning.

What if you are a perfectionist? Are you afraid to try as you want to achieve perfection and fear you won't reach that level? Seeking perfection is pretty much impossible, and instead, we should strive for excellence in all we do. As per a quote from Michael J Fox, "I am careful not to confuse excellence with perfection. Excellence I can reach for; perfection is God's business."

Strive for Excellence, Not Perfection

Most people with grit strive for excellence and do not try to attain perfection. Remember that perfection, in general, is someone else's perception of an ideal standard. This, of course, has its place; for example, in figure skating, there will be an ideal way to execute a jump or spin to meet a required standard. This is often what the judging panel use in a skating competition. The same is true in property and in business, where regulations need to be met to be compliant, keep us all safe, provide a standard and quality control.

However, in general, trying to meet another person's perception of an ideal is like trying to chase their version of success and not yours. This can be a barrier to you being successful and also lead to anxiety and low self-esteem.

Instead, it is advantageous to strive for excellence as an attitude towards your TOP goal. Excellence is derived from the Greek word Arête, which means 'fulfilment of purpose'. For this reason, it is more forgiving to allow for failure to be part of the journey in order to improve and attain excellence, prioritising your progression rather than perfection. Excellence is an attitude, like grit, and these work well together to seek, strive, thrive and achieve.

In property investing, we often see people showing us their property projects, especially wonderful modern-day photography, and we may see perfection. Perhaps you can relate and you know an entrepreneur who has been in business for a while and has some excellent results. However, remember that these are 'excellent' results and seek to strive for that excellence as inspiration. This person would have put in a lot of effort to get to their desired result, and there will be imperfections that you may not see. The same is true for you; striving for excellence is a great way to build your business, brand, and stand out in the business world.

An attitude of excellence also goes hand in hand with being meticulous about what you do, as you are always striving for excellence. So, how does being meticulous help us?

Being Meticulous

Being meticulous is very closely associated with grit. There are, however, two types of being meticulous that I have studied, and your type determines how successful you are.

1. **Achievement-oriented person** – this person works tirelessly to do an excellent job and will want to set goals and try to exceed these goals.

2. **Dependable person** – this is a person who is more conventional and self-controlled. Someone who will show up!

Perhaps you may not be surprised to learn that those who are achievement-oriented achieve more success than those who are dependable people.

If we take a work situation, a dependable person who never steps out of line may not get the same level of success as someone who is more unpredictable, but achievement focused. In the context of figure skating, those who just turn up to practice every day and do exactly what is required will not achieve the success of those who really want to master a move and will practise tirelessly to achieve it, even if they may not be so reliable to work with. The message here is that it is more important to fully strive for excellence or first place than just show up for practice.

I believe there is a balance here. A combination of dependability and achievement orientation go well together, to give amazing results that deliver consistency over time with the desire, hunger and commitment to achieve a TOP goal. In business, this can mean actively pursuing a TOP goal in a focused and tireless way, so that you commit fully to achieving your success. This also means showing up every day, getting up and carrying on no matter what. This last point is also about resilience, which leads me to how grit and resilience work so well together.

Grit and Resilience

We've already discussed resilience in earlier chapters, but it also influences how much grit you have. To be able to control your emotions and recover from difficulties, you need resilience. With grit, you need to have a very strong belief in your reason why, that success and failure lead to growth, and that you have the power to influence your results (you make your own luck).

So, whilst a key component of grit is resilience, resilience is the mechanism that lifts your head up, keeps you moving forward, and helps you be persistent despite any setbacks that you may face. This means that people with grit believe! They believe in their cause and that everything will be ok in the end, and if it is not ok, it is not the end.

Determination and Grit to Take Control

It's great when we feel that we are in control of our behaviour, rather than feeling that external forces have control. Having determination and grit means taking control so that you make choices to shape your future, achieving what you set out to do. This means knowing what you want, making decisions that are right for you, and taking action to make things happen in your business despite any setbacks. When we pursue behaviours that are intrinsically motivating, with extrinsic motivations that are aligned with our TOP goals, we feel happier, more in control, and capable.

Closing Quote

———————

"A man can be as great as he wants to be. If you believe in yourself and have the courage, the determination, the dedication, the competitive drive and if you are willing to sacrifice the little things in life and pay the price for the things that are worthwhile, it can be done."

Vince Lombardi

———————

Exercises: Principle #10

Think about what you decide to spend your free time doing, such as evenings or weekends, and consider the following...

Exercise #1: What Decisions Have You Made Recently?

Write out a list of how you've decided to spend your own time recently.

Example:

Watching TV

Reading a book

_____

_____

_____

_____

_____

Exercise #2: Avoiding Distractions

Identify what your distractions are. List them below.

Example:

Watching a series on TV.

Out to dinner with friends.

_____

_____

_____

_____

_____

Now write down what you are or could be doing instead that would contribute to attaining your TOP goal if you didn't have these distractions?

Example:

Watch a documentary related to your TOP goal.

Listen to a business marketing webinar or podcast.

_____

_____

_____

_____

_____

- Make a list of the advantages and disadvantages to each of the above.

Advantages:

_____

_____

_____

_____

_____

Disadvantages:

_____

_____

_____

_____

_____

- Make a decision on what you will do based on the advantages and disadvantages above. List your decision here:

_____

_____

- How could you schedule the distractions so that you get balance in your life?

_____

_____

_____

_____

_____

Exercise #3: Self-Determination for Problems and Challenges

1. Identify the problem fully – what exactly is the problem that you are facing?

_____

_____

_____

_____

_____

2. Write down as many ideas as you can think of that might help solve the problem.

_____

_____

_____

_____

_____

3. List the pros and cons of each potential solution.

Advantages:

_____

_____

_____

_____

_____

Disadvantages:

_____

_____

_____

_____

4. Choose one of the possible solutions that looks likely to work, based on the pros and cons.

_____

_____

5. Take action! Describe what you will do. Explain your decision.

_____

_____

_____

_____

_____

6. Get another piece of paper and plan out the steps of what you need to do to carry out this solution.

1. _____
2. _____
3. _____
4. _____
5. _____

7. What is your first action/step?

_____

_____

8. Think about your solution... What? When? How? What problems could you encounter? How would you solve them?

_____

_____

_____

_____

_____

After you have executed your solution, consider:

1. Did you achieve what you set out to achieve? If not, how could you change it for next time?

_____

_____

2. Did you achieve progress towards your TOP goal?
    (circle/highlight)

YES/NO

3. What did you learn?

_____

_____

_____

_____

_____

CHAPTER FIFTEEN

———

PRINCIPLE #11: SACRIFICE

Sacrifice is the perfect addition to the ten principles as it brings them all to life. We make sacrifices every day in our decisions and the choices we make reflect the highest values we hold at that time. However, we need to be fully aware of what is most important to us so that we are clear on what to do and the sacrifices we are happy to make to get success. Whether you are a sportsperson, entrepreneur or business owner, there are choices you will make on your journey to prioritise what is aligned to your version of success. This is what is most important to you, and thus foregoing less important, but sometimes very tempting fun activities. Let's explore this further.

What does sacrifice mean?

> ## Definition
>
> **Sacrifice**: Give up (something valued) for the sake of other considerations.

In this context, I believe we could modify this sentence to 'for the sake of other more important considerations.' This is giving up time with friends, relaxing at home reading magazines, perhaps Saturdays watching TV, or lying in on Sunday, to instead spend your time doing other activities and tasks that align more with your vision and TOP goal.

What Does Sacrifice Look Like?

'Success is like an iceberg.' I'm sure you have seen the image before, but it is so true. Sometimes we need reminding that people often just see the success that shows above the water, but what they don't see is all the work required and sacrifices made to achieve this success (below the water). This is true if you are successful in anything you do, in business, in life, as an entrepreneur or an athlete.

To be a high-performing athlete takes hard work, and many choices need to be made every day to be successful. These choices, routines, habits, and the qualities that an athlete incorporates into their everyday life, allows them to achieve their goals and elevates their success above others that are not willing to make the sacrifices required to be the best version of themselves. Athletes learn these great life skills as part of their sport to later apply to all other areas of their life and business.

I have certainly applied the sacrifices that I made to be a high-level figure skater to my property investing business, and this has given me some great results. However, sacrifices to me are something that I have grown up with and are more about choices to be made or what I prioritise in my life, to ultimately get what I value the most. Are you prioritising the tasks that help you towards your TOP goal, at the sacrifice of something of lower value?

Sacrifice or Priority?

To have optimal performance in anything you do starts with you. How well you look after yourself, good habits and routines like those we have worked on during this book, your state of mind, health and wellbeing, as well as skill or knowledge all help to enable success. Eating well, getting up early and taking good care of yourself should be a priority, not a sacrifice.

Working most efficiently and getting the best results in business requires you to be the best version of yourself. This means taking care of your health, fitness, wellbeing, routines, thoughts and beliefs so that you are in a fit state of mind and body to grow your business.

Tip #28: Take good care of you first so that you can take good care of your business.

Making choices on what you decide to do that will benefit you the most, should also be a priority rather than a sacrifice, as this will lead you to the life you have clearly defined on your vision board. This is about prioritising what you want the most—your business goals—by giving up something that is valued, but of less value to you.

Once you have prioritised you, the next question is what to do with the limited time you have to ensure that you are working towards that TOP goal that will bring you the success you desire. Time is one thing we can never get more of, so it is very important that we use it wisely and most efficiently to get the best results.

Time Sacrifices

To become a high-level athlete takes a great deal of practice time. For me, this was sometimes twice a day, early before school at 5 am, after school and at the weekend. The top athletes that I was surrounded by would train for 25-45 hours per week, which is the equivalent to most people's work week. Time that athletes could otherwise spend with friends, family, doing other activities or on holiday. However, these are the type of sacrifices made to be a top athlete.

Likewise, property investing, or starting and scaling any business, also takes time, especially at the start. When starting out, I was on-site at weekends and evenings to get a property ready for tenants to move in. You need to be willing to make these types of sacrifices in your business in order to meet deadlines, fix issues and get the business started. You may also find that sometimes you have to work more on your business than the 'normal' working hours of a job. Spending time on your business will mean that you will have less time to spend doing other activities, so a time sacrifice is required in the short term for longer-term gain.

As mentioned above, time is also the one thing that we can never get back, so it is very important to use your time in the best way possible. Ensure that you spend your time wisely. Focus on the activities that are of greatest value to you, that help you achieve your vision and with close friends, family, and like-minded people.

Tip #29: Time is one thing you can never get back, so it's important to use it wisely.

Financial Sacrifices

To be an athlete at any level costs money, from paying for lessons to having the required equipment. The investment in my figure skating was an expense that my parents paid, and this would have been several thousands of pounds per year. I am grateful that my parents were able to support me in this way. However, it did mean that I chose to have skating presents instead of other presents—skating boots or dresses as opposed to the latest Nintendo that may have been popular at the time. Figure skating was more important in my life, so skating equipment would be the best present. It is worth considering your spending choices, as sacrifices in other areas of your life are often required to finance what is most important to you.

Regarding finances in my life now, if I had to—which was certainly true at the start of my property journey—I would sacrifice a new car to buy a house. That is because I prioritise appreciating assets over depreciating assets. Appreciating assets are assets that go up in value over time and are often bought as part of an investing strategy like property investing, whilst depreciating assets decline in value. Below I have included some examples of appreciating and depreciating assets:

Examples of appreciating assets: houses, bonds, savings accounts.

Examples of depreciating assets: motor vehicles, furniture, equipment, plant, and machinery.

In the exercise section at the end of this chapter, there is an assets table for you to complete and a good debt versus bad debt sheet for you to consider.

Good and Bad Debt

Good debt is borrowing money that has the potential to increase your net worth. Bad debt is borrowing money to purchase depreciating assets. The rule is that if an asset won't go up in value or generate income, then you really should not go into debt to buy it.

Example of good debt: mortgage or student loans.

Example of bad debt: store cards or car loans.

To increase our net worth and grow our business, we may need to make a short-term sacrifice of not buying a new pair of shoes or using a credit card to buy a new TV. In future, with an increased net worth, we can afford to buy depreciating assets that we really love.

Sacrifice in Life

Robert Kiyosaki, the author of Rich Dad Poor Dad, often spoke to people about investing in property, and the most common response he would receive was, "I don't want to fix toilets." Property investing can be a lucrative business, so what Robert Kiyosaki understood this to mean was that these people were giving smaller problems, like fixing toilets, of greater importance than building a profitable property portfolio, having financial independence and lifestyle choices.

It's worth considering here that the level of sacrifice you make is proportionate to your level of success, so if you are unwilling to sacrifice your social life, time, comforts, or even pride, then you will struggle to reach the level of success that you desire.

A sacrifice in figure skating would be getting up at 4 a.m. in the morning during the winter months, when it was freezing cold and dark outside, to have an empty ice-rink and get some quality focused practice. This would impact my social life, but this was a sacrifice I was willing to make to be the best I could be at a sport I loved. I apply this directly to property investing in getting purposeful work completed at the start of the day, basically getting up early to get ahead. It's also possible to accomplish focused work in those early hours before anyone has started their day.

If you had to, would you be willing to give up sleeping in to become your version of successful? Getting up early to devote time working on income-generating tasks so you can fulfil your TOP goal that gets you closer to success?

What Would You Sacrifice to Get Your Version of Success?

Getting the success you defined earlier in Chapter Seven will require you to give up other things and make choices. Perhaps if you enjoy watching TV, you would need to sacrifice this to spend your time creating the vision board from Chapter Five Be honest and ask yourself, are you willing to do this to achieve your goals? How important is your vision, desire and reason why? How much are you realistically willing to sacrifice to achieve your version of success?

The exercises at the end of this chapter will help you understand your level of sacrifice.

Levels of Sacrifice

I believe sacrifice comes in many forms and levels. As mentioned earlier, whether you are a recreational sportsperson, an amateur, a professional, elite or Olympic athlete, sacrifices have to be made at each level, and life lessons are learned throughout. The level of sacrifice of an Olympic athlete can be massive. Finding the level of sacrifice that you are prepared to make should always be a consideration in your life, so that you achieve the right balance that is aligned to your version of success. I know what sacrifices I will make to achieve my vision and my version of success. The question is, what will be your level of sacrifice to achieve your vision and your version of success?

Tip #30: Know the level of sacrifice that you are willing make in your life to get your version of success.

It is not easy to commit to a level of sacrifice, but your success requires your sacrifice.

Closing Quotes

"Being an athlete is a lifestyle that consumes every aspect of your life. Whether you're a professional athlete, recreational athlete or participate in sport while you're in school. You'll have to make all kinds of sacrifices in order to succeed. It's important to surround yourself with a strong support system – people who understand your desire to be the best and will support you through thick and thin."

Melodie Anne

"Your level of success will rarely exceed your level of personal development, because success is something you attract by the person you become."

Hal Elrod

"If you want to live an exceptional and extraordinary life, you have to give up many of the things that are part of a normal one."

Srinivas Rao

"He who would accomplish little must sacrifice little; he who would achieve much must sacrifice much; he who would attain highly must sacrifice greatly."

James Allen

Exercises: Principle #11

Exercise #1: Social and Time Sacrifice for Your Vision and Your Success

1. What is one thing you would sacrifice to achieve your vision?

   _____

   _____

2. How would you spend the time instead to achieve your vision?

   _____

   _____

   _____

   _____

   _____

Exercise #2: Financial Sacrifice

List out your appreciating assets:

_____

_____

_____

_____

_____

List out your depreciating assets:

_____

_____

_____

_____

_____

List out your good debt:

_____

_____

_____

_____

_____

List out your bad debt:

_____

_____

_____

_____

_____

What do you have more of? Ideally you would have more good debt and more appreciating assets.

_____

_____

_____

_____

_____

Are you spending to your means? (circle of highlight)

YES/NO?

Exercise #3: Financial Lifestyle Budget

Complete the financial lifestyle budget below to find out how to live to your means and beyond to get financial independence.

Financial Lifestyle Budget

Your income: _____

Costs: _____

Bills _____

    Car _____

    Phone _____

    Groceries _____

    Gym _____

    Childcare _____

    Subscriptions _____

    Entertainment _____

    Shopping _____

    Going Out _____

    Holidays/travelling _____

    Misc _____

How much money would you need to replace your income?

_____

How much money do you need to survive on?

_____

How much money do you have if you had no income tomorrow?

_____

Consider what plans you can make for your future to increase your net-worth, income and minimise bad debt so you can achieve your goals.

The electronic version of the financial lifestyle budget is available in the playbook here: www.stateofmindplaybook.com.

CHAPTER SIXTEEN

FINAL THOUGHTS

If you have read to the end of this book, then I believe that you have realised that there are no hidden secrets or magic formulae for success in business or sport. Acquiring knowledge or skill is essential, but what is equally important is how you balance the equation of state of mind and knowledge to achieve your goals. Remember, research shows that 80% of what you achieve is about your state of mind. In fact, I think the real BIG secret is that I am not special, and you can achieve whatever it is that you want. I don't believe there is a genius for entrepreneurship, but a lot of effort and smart work is certainly required to master the knowledge and state of mind to get the results you desire. The ability to be able to grow your state of mind to be the best version of yourself, so that you can take action to be successful.

Sportsperson to Property Entrepreneur

It has taken me many years of figure skating as a child, being a professional coach, in-depth research and, of course, growing my property business to learn and develop these state of mind principles that have helped me be my version of successful. I never knew that I was learning these principles as a young athlete, but I am forever grateful for this experience that taught me so much. Once I started asking the question, 'What makes the difference?' to achieve success and researched this in sport and entrepreneurship, I was able to identify the principles that help achieve results. The good news is, I have put all the principles together in one place for you to accelerate your learning much faster than mine. It will, of course, take time; this is not an overnight success method, but I have done all the hard work for you. I have given you all the learnings, exercises and tips from extensive research as a qualified coach and mentor, 35 years of sport, 15 years as a professional ice-skating coach and 9 years of running a successful property investing business, so that you can use these state of mind principles straight away to take action and accelerate your business journey.

Knowledge Without State of Mind

I too, was fearful when I first started my own business. Still, my state of mind skillset helped me get out of my comfort zone, take action, and overcome the many challenges in property investing and business. I find it saddening when I see property investors and entrepreneurs alike, who have all the knowledge but struggle with the state of mind to take action. There are so many I have met, and in all situations, it's not worth them having the knowledge if they do not do anything about it. In most cases, these people are held back by fear; they perhaps don't know their reason, lack self-belief, and don't know where to start with their knowledge. This may be because they have not mastered the state of mind needed to take action to build a business that is right for them, their vision, desire and reason, and ultimately their success.

I wrote this book to help you adopt that 80% state of mind from sport that starts with YOU and really does make the difference, so that you DO take action to get results in your business.

You can do it!

You can learn the principles in this book as I have done and apply them to your business. As I mentioned, right at the very start, these principles are not innate, meaning we were not born with them, so anyone can learn them. I was fortunate enough for sport to teach me, but you can do it too. I really do believe that people can change their lives if they choose to and have the right state of mind to achieve their version of success. I believe in you, and I believe that with the state of mind blueprint, anyone can be successful.

Will You Take Action?

I believe in you, but the key question is, do you believe in you? If not, then do ensure that you re-read the self-belief chapter. If you don't work on your state of mind to achieve your vision, then no one will do it for you. You need to create routines, be resilient, persistent, have a growth state of mind and make those sacrifices to reach your goals. The action has to come from you. Sometimes the first step can be the hardest, so that's where being clear in the first principle of this book on your reason and desire is the perfect starting point to propel you forward. Then you can start taking steps on your journey because you are clear on what you are doing and why you are doing it. I hope you have done this already, as we have reached the end of the book, but if not, then it is never too late; you can use this book any time you need it. If you are still unclear on your reason why, ensure you do Chapter Five first and don't move on until you've mastered your passion and you have clarity on your reason and desire. This will fuel the rest of your journey and enable the other principles to align with your core value system. If you don't do this first, you may find yourself lost and not knowing who you are, what you are doing or where to start.

Please keep this book as a 'living' reference book.

As we mentioned earlier, your mind needs exercise like a muscle to reach its ideal state. The state of mind blueprint can be referred to whenever you need it in your business journey. The exercises within this book can be used any time, and if you need help in one particular area, for example routine, you can just review that chapter and complete the exercises to help you. Don't forget to be clear on your reason, though! If you need to update your vision and your goals as you have changed, you can use this book for help by following the process defined in the relevant chapter.

Remember if you haven't done so already, you also have the State of Mind Playbook available for you to download. It's free and has all the exercises and templates from this book in an easy format for electronic use or a printable version. Go to www.stateofmindplaybook.com.

BONUS TIP

Tip #31: Ensure you know your reason why and desire first and foremost.

Remember...

- Use your thoughts and beliefs to empower you to get results.
- The success iceberg analogy!
- Achieving your goals takes time; make sure you enjoy the journey.
- Know your reason and desire to keep you moving towards your TOP goal.
- The best time to start is now, if you haven't started already... start NOW!

At the start of the book, I mentioned that if you learned these principles and applied them to your business as I have done in a way that works for you, then you could achieve your version of success, enjoy your journey and be a better version of you. I still believe that is true. The magic is that that no one is special, I don't have any unfair advantage and if I can achieve my version of success, you can achieve yours.

Final Quote

Most of those who have achieved success would have worked extremely hard to get there, and many of them may even have been told that they would never amount to anything. However, these people believed that they could achieve and would have worked tirelessly to do so. Believe to achieve!

———

"The moment that we believe that success is determined by an ingrained level of ability, we will be brittle in the face of adversity."

Josh Waitzkin

- Chess Grandmaster and Martial Artist

———

REFERENCES

Introduction:

Definition of 'state', Cambridge Dictionary,
https://dictionary.cambridge.org/dictionary/english/state

Chapter 1:

Buster Douglas, Wikipedia, https://en.wikipedia.org/wiki/Buster_Douglas

Calvin Brock, Wikipedia, https://en.wikipedia.org/wiki/Calvin_Brock

Catherine Clifford, CNBC, https://www.cnbc.com/2017/03/03/venus-williams-why-athletes-make-great-entrepreneurs.html

Dan Robinson, NS Business, https://www.ns-businesshub.com/business/footballers-in-business/

David Lloyd, Wikipedia, https://en.wikipedia.org/wiki/David_Lloyd_(tennis)

Derek Jeter, Wikipedia, https://en.wikipedia.org/wiki/Derek_Jeter

Entrepeneur, Derek Jeter on What Motivates Him, https://www.entrepreneur.com/article/306524

Entrepreneur, 30 Legendary Athletes Who Became Business All-Stars. https://www.entrepreneur.com/slideshow/305571

GDA Speakers, https://www.gdaspeakers.com/speaker/patrick-sweeney/

George Foreman, https://www.georgeforeman.co.uk

George Foreman, Wikipedia,

https://en.wikipedia.org/wiki/George_Foreman

Habit Stacker, 24 Motivational Kobe Bryant Quotes,

https://thehabitstacker.com/24-motivational-kobe-bryant-quotes/

Jack and Landlords, https://www.jackandlandlords.com

Kobe Bryant, Wikipedia, https://en.wikipedia.org/wiki/Kobe_Bryant

Kristi Yamaguchi, Wikipedia,

https://en.wikipedia.org/wiki/Kristi_Yamaguchi

Maria Sharapova, Wikipedia,

https://en.wikipedia.org/wiki/Maria_Sharapova

Patrick Sweeney, Wikipedia,

https://en.wikipedia.org/wiki/Patrick_Sweeney_(entrepreneur)

Robbie Fowler, Wikipedia, https://en.wikipedia.org/wiki/Robbie_Fowler

Todd Stottlemyre, Wikipedia,

https://en.wikipedia.org/wiki/Todd_Stottlemyre

Venus Williams, Wikipedia, https://en.wikipedia.org/wiki/Venus_Williams

Wired For Youth, Discipline Equals Freedom by Jocko Willink,

https://wiredforyouth.com/summaries/discipline-equals-freedom-by-jocko-willink-book-summary-notes-and-pdf/

Yitzi Weiner, Medium, https://medium.com/thrive-global/29-pro-athletes-who-became-entrepreneurs-and-how-they-are-still-winning-out-of-the-stadium-dfef5e06c9bf

Chapter 2:

The Man Who Thinks He Can poem:

Roger Edwards, *The Little Things & Such: Motivational Poems You Know and Love Now with Reflection Questions*, (Independently Published, 2013)

Walter D. Wintle, "Thinking", *Unity* (Unity Tract Society, 1905)

Early publications of this poem cite Walter D. Wintle as being the author. Later sources gave this poem, which originally carried the title 'Thinking', 'The Man Who Thinks He Can' and 'It's All In The State Of Mind'.

Chapter 3:

Definition of 'thought', Lexico,
https://www.lexico.com/definition/thought

Alison Flynn, Elizabeth Campbell and et al, *Growth & Goals: a course-integrated module to better equip students with learning skills*, Open Library PressBooks,
https://ecampusontario.pressbooks.pub/growthandgoalscourse/chapter/what-is-a-mindset/
Carol S. Dweck, *Mindset: The New Psychology of Success; How We Can Learn To Fulfil Our Potential* (Gildan Media Corp, 2007)
Christine Comaford, *Got Inner Peace? 5 Ways To Get It NOW*, Forbes,
https://www.forbes.com/sites/christinecomaford/2012/04/04/got-inner-peace-5-ways-to-get-it-now/#2c6177ad6672
J. D. Meier, *What is Mindset?*, Sources of Insight,
https://sourcesofinsight.com/what-is-mindset/
Jannie, Johnson, *Racial Unrest Is Deeper than....Skin/Color*, Jackson Advocate, p. 8A, vol. 82, no. 39 (Jackson Advocate, 25 June 2020)
MindsetWorks, http://www.mindsetworks.com
MSP Marketing, *No Brain, No Gain! Breaking MSP Marketing Plateaus in 2021*, Your Sales Energy, https://yoursalesenergy.com/msp-marketing-2021/
Ralph Lewis, *What Actually Is a Thought? And How Is Information*, Psychology

Today, https://www.psychologytoday.com/us/blog/finding-purpose/201902/what-actually-is-thought-and-how-is-information-physical

Skeptic Forum, *Belief (not just religious belief) ought to be abolished*, https://www.skepticforum.com/viewtopic.php?t=29250&start=80

Sonya Mann, *Tony Robbins Says Success Is Only 20 Percent Skill and the Rest Is All in Your Head*, Inc, https://www.inc.com/sonya-mann/tony-robbins-says-entrepreneurship-is-not-for-everyone.html

Tony Robbins, *The Psychology Of A Winner*, https://www.tonyrobbins.com/stories/coaching/the-psychology-of-a-winner/

Chapter 4:

Definition of 'desire', Lexico, https://www.lexico.com/definition/desire and Dictionary.com, https://www.dictionary.com/

Harrison Barnes, You Need to Have Desire to Achieve Your Goals (2022), https://www.harrisonbarnes.com/you-need-to-have-desire-to-achieve-your-goals/

Stanford Encyclopedia of Philosophy, *Desire* (2009, updated 2015) https://plato.stanford.edu/entries/desire/

University of Cambridge, *Vroom's Expectancy Theory*, https://www.ifm.eng.cam.ac.uk/research/dstools/vrooms-expectancy-theory/

Victor H. Vroom, Deci, E.L., *Management and Motivation*, Vroom, (Penguin 1983, first published 1970)

Quote by Marsha Sinetar, https://www.brainyquote.com/quotes/marsha_sinetar_401280

Chapter 6:

Definition of 'goal', Lexico, https://www.lexico.com/definition/goal

Definition of 'goal-oriented', Dictionary.com, https://www.dictionary.com/browse/goal-oriented

Eva V. Monsma, *Principles of Effective Goal Setting*, Association for Applied Sport Psychology, https://appliedsportpsych.org/resources/resources-for-athletes/principles-of-effective-goal-setting/

Goal Orientation, Wikipedia, https://en.wikipedia.org/wiki/Goal_orientation

Goal Setting for Synchronized Skaters and Coaches: Self-determining what you can achieve! Synchronized Skating Magazine (May, 2007)

James Clear, *Atomic Habits* (Random House Business, 2018)

Matthew Syed, *Bounce* (Fourth Estate, 2011)

SMART Criteria, Wikipedia, https://en.wikipedia.org/wiki/SMART_criteria

Sport Information Resource Centre, *Goal Orientations: task vs. ego* (2014), http://sircsportresearch.blogspot.com/2014/05/goal-orientations-task-vs-ego.html#axzz6cMsQ9e6B

Stephen R. Covey, *The Seven Habits of Highly Effective People* (Simon & Schuster, 2004)

W. Davis, C. Carson, A. Ammeter, D. Treadway, *The Interactive Effects of Goal Orientation and Feedback Specificity on Task Performance* (Human Performance, October 2005; 18(4): 409-426)

Quote by Albert Einstein, https://www.quotespedia.org/authors/a/albert-einstein/if-you-want-to-live-a-happy-life-tie-it-to-a-goal-not-to-people-or-things-albert-einstein/

Chapter 7:

Definition of 'routine', Lexico, https://www.lexico.com/definition/routine

Definition of 'habit', Merriam-Webster, https://www.merriam-webster.com/dictionary/habit

Charles Duhigg, *The Power of Habit: Why We Do What We Do, and How to Change*, (Random House Books, 2013)

James Clear, *Atomic Habits* (Random House Business, 2018)

Pete Ross, *The Importance of Routine for Peak Athletic Performance*, Medium, https://pwross.medium.com/the-importance-of-routine-for-peak-athletic-performance-375bb2c49f40

Peter W Ross, *Building The Elite Athlete: The Complete Guide to Achieving Your Full Athletic* (Independently Published, 2019)

Quote by Mike Murdock, https://www.brainyquote.com/quotes/mike_murdock_185322

Chapter 8:

Definition of 'success', Cambridge Dictionary, https://dictionary.cambridge.org/dictionary/english/success

Definition of 'mistake', Cambridge Dictionary, https://dictionary.cambridge.org/dictionary/english/mistake

Amy Morin, *5 Ways To Turn Your Mistake Into A Valuable Life Lesson*, Forbes, https://www.forbes.com/sites/amymorin/2017/07/17/5-ways-to-turn-your-mistake-into-a-valuable-life-lesson/?sh=5b7dd8001c01

Elizabeth Day, *How to Fail: Everything I've Ever Learned from Things Going Wrong* (Fourth Estate, 2018)

Tim Ferris, *Tools of Titans: The Tactics, Routines, and Habits of Billionaires, Icons, and World-Class Performers* (Vermilion, 2017)

Chapter 9:

Definition of 'persistence', Lexico,
https://www.lexico.com/definition/persistence

Al Siebert, *The Resiliency Advantage: Master Change, Thrive Under Pressure, and Bounce Back from Setbacks* (Berrett-Koehler Publishers, 2005)

American Psychological Association, *Building Your Resilience*, https://www.apa.org/topics/resilience

Barbara Fredrickson, *Positivity: Ground breaking Research To Release You Inner Optimist And Thrive* (Harmony, 2009)

Growing Resilient, *3 P's*, http://growingresilient.com/home/tools/3-ps/

History of SpaceX, Wikipedia, https://en.wikipedia.org/wiki/History_of_SpaceX

Martin Seligman, *Learned Optimism: How to Change Your Mind and Your Life* (Nicholas Brealey Publishing, 2006)

Mindspurt, *Why And How To Be A Persistent Person To Achieve Success*, https://mindspurt.com/2018/11/13/why-and-how-to-be-a-persistent-person-to-achieve-success/

Positive Psychology, *What is Resilience and Why is It Important to Bounce Back?*, https://positivepsychology.com/what-is-resilience/

Rick Hanson, *Resilient: How to Grow an Unshakable Core of Calm, Strength, and Happiness* (Ebury Digital, 2018)

Steven M Southwick and Dennis S Charney, *Resilience: The Science of Mastering Life's Greatest Challenges* (Cambridge University Press, 2018)

Chapter 10:

Definition of 'realism', Lexico, https://www.lexico.com/definition/realism

Courtney E. Ackerman, *What is Positive Mindset: 89 Ways to Achieve a Positive Mental Attitude*, Positive Psychology,

https://positivepsychology.com/positive-mindset/

E. R. James, *Positive Mindset: What is a positive mindset?*, Your Talent Your Wealth, https://www.yourtalentyourwealth.com/positive-mindsetwhat-is-a-positive-mindset/

Chapter 11:

Definition for 'self-confidence', Genevieve Freeman,

https://freemanlifecoach.com/news/

Definition of 'self-worth', Merriam-Webster, https://www.merriam-webster.com/dictionary/self-worth and Lexico,

https://www.lexico.com/definition/self-esteem

Caroline Castrillon, *5 Ways To Go From A Scarcity To Abundance Mindset*, Forbes, https://www.forbes.com/sites/carolinecastrillon/2020/07/12/5-ways-to-go-from-a-scarcity-to-abundance-mindset/#5c2d8a241197

Courtney E. Ackerman, *12 Tips For Building Self-Confidence and Self-Belief*, Positive Psychology, https://positivepsychology.com/self-confidence-self-belief/

Courtney E. Ackerman, *What is Self-Worth and How Do We Increase it?*, Positive Psychology, https://positivepsychology.com/self-worth/

Ginger Dean, *4 Ways To Shift Your Money Mindset From Scarcity To Abundance*, Forbes, https://www.forbes.com/sites/gingerdean/2017/12/31/4-ways-to-shift-your-money-mindset-from-scarcity-to-abundance/#561a0da53a37

Kristin Neff, *Self-Compassion: The Proven Power of Being Kind to Yourself* (Yellow Kite, 2011)

MindTools, *How To Build Self-Confidence*,

https://www.mindtools.com/selfconf.html

Stephen R. Covey, *The Seven Habits of Highly Effective People* (Simon & Schuster, 2004)

Chapter 12:

Comfort Zone, Wikipedia, https://en.wikipedia.org/wiki/Comfort_zone
Harvard Medical School, Understanding the Stress Response, Harvard Health Publishing, https://www.health.harvard.edu/staying-healthy/understanding-the-stress-response
Jennifer Cumming, Sport Imagery Training, Association for Applied Sport Psychology, https://appliedsportpsych.org/resources/resources-for-athletes/sport-imagery-training/

Chapter 13:

Definition for 'motivation', Wikipedia,
https://en.wikipedia.org/wiki/Motivation

Catherine Moore, *What is Flow in Psychology?*, Positive Psychology,
https://positivepsychology.com/what-is-flow/
Comfort Zone, Wikipedia, https://en.wikipedia.org/wiki/Comfort_zone
David G. Myers, *Psychology in Modules*, eighth edition (Worth Publishers, 2007)
Flow (psychology), Wikipedia,
https://en.wikipedia.org/wiki/Flow_(psychology)
James Clear, *Motivation: The Scientific Guide on How to Get and Stay Motivated,*
www.jamesclear.com/motivation
Kendra Cherry, *Extrinsic vs. Intrinsic Motivation: What's the difference?*, Very Well Mind, https://www.verywellmind.com/differences-between-extrinsic-and-intrinsic-motivation-2795384

Mihaly Csikszentmihalyi, *Flow and the Foundations of Positive Psychology: The Collected Works of Mihaly Csikszentmihalyi* (Springer, 2014)

Mike Oppland, *8 Ways To Create Flow According to Mihaly Csikszentmihalyi*, Positive Psychology, https://positivepsychology.com/mihaly-csikszentmihalyi-father-of-flow/

Robert Weinberg and Daniel Gould, *Foundations of Sport and Exercise Psychology*, sixth edition (Human Kinetics, 2015)

Steven Pressfield, *The War of Art* (Black Irish Entertainment, 2012)

Chapter 14:

Definition of 'determination', Lexico, https://www.lexico.com/definition/determination

Andrew Zolli and Ann Marie Healy, *Resilience: Why Things Bounce Back* (Headline, 2012)

Angela Duckworth, *Grit: The Power of Passion and Perseverance* (Ebury Digital, 2016)

Janice Almond, *BEING DETERMINED: How to be Relentless in Pursuing Your Dreams in 15 Simple Ways*, volume 2, (Zion Publishing House, 2016)

Margaret Perlis, *5 Characteristics of Grit, What It Is, Why You Need It and Do You Have It*, Forbes, https://www.forbes.com/sites/margaretperlis/2013/10/29/5-characteristics-of-grit-what-it-is-why-you-need-it-and-do-you-have-it/?sh=4982df0c4f7b

Malcolm Gladwell, *Outliers* (Penguin, 2009)

Matthew Syed, *Bounce: The Myth of Talent and the Power of Practice* (Fourth Estate, 2010)

Chapter 15:

Definition of 'sacrifice', Lexico,
https://www.lexico.com/definition/sacrifice

Hal Elrod, *The Miracle Morning* (Hal Elrod, 2012)
Robert Kiyosaki and Sharon Lechter, Rich Dad Poor Dad (Plata Publishing, 1997)

Chapter 16:

Skills You Need, *The Importance of Mindset*,
https://www.skillsyouneed.com/ps/mindsets.html

ABOUT THE AUTHOR

Wendy lives in Almondsbury near Bristol with her husband and property dog Lucca in their self-build home.

Before she started writing, Wendy was a sportsperson, a computer science graduate and a project management consultant. She then found the wonderful world of property investing and is now a full-time property entrepreneur, keynote speaker, coach and mentor. Fascinated by what makes people succeed, Wendy spent many years studying top athletes and entrepreneurs noting down the key success principles you will find in this book.

When she is not writing, speaking or investing, Wendy loves running, going on long walks with Lucca, travelling and spending time with family.

Keep in touch with Wendy:

Website: www.wendybrumwell.com

Instagram: www.instagram.com/wendyemmabrumwell

LinkedIn: www.linkedin.com/in/wendybrumwell/

A Successful State Of Mind:

www.asuccessfulstateofmind.com

Download the State Of Mind Playbook:

www.stateofmindplaybook.com

Printed in Great Britain
by Amazon

50419884R00158